Debt Sentence

How Canada's Student Loan System is Failing Young People and the Country

Thomas F. Pawlick

Copyright © 2012 Thomas F. Pawlick

ISBN 978-1-62141-779-8

All rights reserved. No part of this publication may be reproduced, stored in a retrieval system, or transmitted in any form or by any means, electronic, mechanical, recording or otherwise, without the prior written permission of the author.

Published by BookLocker.com, Inc., Bradenton, Florida.

Printed in the United States of America on acid-free paper.

BookLocker.com, Inc.
2012

First Edition

for

Marguerite Therese

Music Box Dancer

Contents

Introduction: A Lost World 1

Chapter One: Eating Our Young 5
Thirty nine reasons why Canada's student loans system is a disaster.

Chapter Two: "You reach a number, and you're out...." .. 21
A story that is not at all unusual, of personal and national loss.

Chapter Three: Tales from Neverland 45
Canadian students speak out--loudly--3,000 times a day.

Chapter Four: Easy Meals 77
How the system treats people with disabilities.

Chapter Five: Collateral Damage 103
Canadian society takes multiple hits, from hospitals to courtrooms.

Chapter Six: Who's (who) on First 129
The history, politics, companies and people behind the system.

Chapter Seven: BMOC (Big Money on Campus) 179
How commercialization affects the hallowed Halls of Academe.

Chapter Eight: "The population wants it." 201
How other countries handle higher education, and how Canada might do so.

Chapter Nine: Sources, Tools, Allies 231
Further information and sources of help for borrowers.

Introduction: A Lost World

A group of students gathered round my desk after class, to ask questions about the lecture I'd just given. They were good kids, bright, idealistic, refreshingly open. After a 28-year career in journalism, I'd recently returned to teaching, and the genuine pleasure of spending time with these young people was daily confirming that my decision was a good one.

Then a student, a girl whose sense of humor and sharp wit often enlivened class discussions, asked a question I hadn't yet heard. "Professor Pawlick," she said, this time serious, "when you got your bachelor's degree, what was your student loan debt?"

Debt?

What was she talking about?

I earned my bachelor's degree in 1965, back in the Movement Years. Mine took longer than most, because I'd switched majors and universities in midstream, and took an extra year to go to France and study at the Universite de Poitiers. All-told my bachelor's took six years, plus an additional year in graduate school to get my teaching certification. Seven years.

My father had offered to help, but I wanted to pay my own way, and did. The auto industry was booming then, and jobs were plentiful along the Detroit/Windsor border. Summers I worked at the Jones and Dabney auto paint plant in Detroit, inhaling fumes and getting splashed in a wide variety of colors. During the school year, I worked evenings and Saturdays in a department store, selling sheet music and 33-1/3 wax albums in the music department. It was enough to pay for tuition and books, living expenses and entertainment, and for a used Ford two-door, painted in Henry Ford's favorite color: black. The year in France had cost me–no, I'm not making this up–a total of $1,000.

Debt? I had no debts then, until marriage came along and we put a down payment on a small, cracker-box house and took out a mortgage. That was debt.

When, in my 50s, I took education leave from my job and went back to school to earn a graduate degree at Carleton University in Ottawa, it was paid for by my then-employers. They'd also covered my children's undergraduate courses. Of school debt, until then, I was blissfully ignorant.

Over the next several years, my students educated me, showing me their own far different reality.

It was grim, almost Dickensian. Looking at their situation, I could only marvel at how the academic world had changed for the worse, and that in spite of it they were still so hopeful, so idealistic. In their shoes, I'd never have stuck it out. I'd have quit school and gone to work full-time on the assembly line at Jones and Dabney. The student life I'd known was now a Lost World.

Gradually, this began to grate on me. It was unfair, unjust. Why should the generation I was teaching be so heavily penalized, compared to those who'd preceded them? Hard case after hard case filed in and out of my classes, as I watched in dismay. Finally, my own daughter, who'd been enrolled in a doctoral program, was caught in the gears. Irritation turned to outrage.

And then to the decision to write this book.

My first stop was a day-long meeting with the Canadian Federation of Students' President, David Molenhuis, CFS National Researcher Graham Cox, and Austin Miller, president of the Graduate Students Association at my alma mater,

Carleton. What they told me deepened my revulsion at the present system, and provided a framework for subsequent research.

What that research found begins with Chapter one.

In what follows, many students speak. Some have bravely allowed their names to be used, while others have requested that they not be. In some cases, even when a student was willing to give a name, I've left it out or used a fictitious name anyway, to protect them. At their age, and in their position, young people are very vulnerable. No one knows this better than a teacher.

In other cases, I've also left out the names of individual banks, collection agencies or other entities, not because they don't deserve opprobrium, but simply because singling one out over all the others might make it look like their competitors were innocent. They aren't. The practices students and graduates describe are pretty much industry-wide. I could as easily have substituted any familiar corporate name for another, since most would have done the same.

The greatest responsibility for the evils of the present system rests with those governments, both federal and provincial, which have the power to protect the interests of Canada's youth, but don't.

Ed. Note: Among the sources cited in the endnotes to each chapter of this book are several references to the famed *Wikipedia*. Some academics frown on the *Wikipedia* as "unreliable" and not "authoritative." However, in every case where I've used it in the past, it has proven accurate. Much like the Occupy Movement currently capturing headlines, it is an entirely democratic endeavor–the very opposite of elitism. No media baron or corporate PR flack can post anything on it without fear of near-immediate correction. Nor can any well-meaning but heavy handed spokesperson for the left. All of us help to keep it honest.

I like that idea, and quote from Wiki sources freely.

Chapter One: Eating Our Young

"thy desires are wolvish, bloody, starved and ravenous."

--Shakespeare, *The Merchant of Venice*

Filial cannibalism, the practice of killing and eating one's own or one's neighbor's young, is relatively rare among mammals. It usually crops up in desperate cases, where a species is facing starvation, or in situations where genetic dominance is the evolutionary goal.

Rodent species that reproduce very quickly, like mice, voles or Norway rats, may occasionally make too much whoopee, and the resulting overproduction and crowding may lead to hungry, over-stressed individuals eating the results. Male African lions, when they take over a new pride of females, may kill off the young of any rival males, to assure their own leadership dominance.

However, for animals to destroy not only the young of leadership rivals, but their own offspring, and not only in times of scarcity but in times of plenty and abundant resources, is almost unheard of.

Except, that is, in Canada and the U.S.A., where humans have created a phenomenon called the Student Loan System.

Over the past 25 years or so, this entity, starting from small, almost innocuous, beginnings, has grown into the sort of creature normally encountered only in the scripts of science fiction writers: an invisible, yet monstrous devourer of all things educational, and especially of those seeking an education. It has become the strongest arm in an overall push to privatize not only our university and community college campuses, but education at all levels.

Based on a simplistic market ideology, this drive to privatize is tainting the nature of our post-secondary institutions, altering their budgets, their curriculae, and the philosophies on which they were originally based. It has contributed to a takeover by for-profit companies not only of government's practical jurisdiction over education in particular, but of many of government's basic functions, from dictating public policy and staffing government departments, to printing and distributing government publications–including those describing the loans system itself.

It skews the structure of our society, and is seriously compromising our future. It is ruining the lives of an entire generation–our children–by forcing them into a form of debt peonage that poses perhaps the most serious threat we've seen so far to the social and financial health of our nation.

The problem is massive—according to the Canadian Association of University Teachers there were more than 1.7 million students enrolled in Canada's universities and community colleges in 2008/2009,[1] and the number has only grown since.

But getting an exact numerical fix on their financial situation can be difficult. For example, the Canadian Federation of Students has reported that:

"In September 2010 the total amount of student loans owed to the [federal] government reached $15 billion, the legislative ceiling set by the Canada Student Financial Assistance Act. In response, the government altered the definition of 'student loan' to exclude over $1.5 billion in federal student debt..... In addition, the $15 billion figure actually only accounts for a portion of Canada's total education-related debt, as it does not include provincial and personal loans, lines of credit and credit card debt."[2]

According to the federation, the federal Canada Student Loan Program (CSLP) alone expected "to lend approximately $2.1 billion during the 2010-2011 academic year."[3] And the rate of loan uptake is projected to rise steeply, from 36 per cent in 2008-09 to 51 per cent in 2033-34.[4]

As long ago as 2006, more than 59 per cent of students graduating with a bachelor's degree had significant debt burdens, averaging $24,047 per student.[5] The figures are higher today, and the interest being charged on those loans is unsustainable.

A 2007 report by the Coalition for Student Loan Fairness showed that Canadian student loan interest was "more than double charged by most countries."[6] While the federal government borrowed money to fund its loan program at "an average rate of 4.45 per cent, when students repay the loans, starting six months after graduation, they pay between 8.5 and 11 per cent interest." In contrast, Germany and New Zealand charge no interest on student loans, while "the United States charge only about 3.37 per cent."[7]

When the so-called "sub-prime mortgage bubble" burst beyond the bounds of the real estate sector, it nearly plunged the world into a second Great Depression. What might happen when the student loan bubble is pierced?

A historic shift

It wasn't always thus. From 1939 to 1964, government funding of post-secondary education in Canada came under the Dominion-Provincial Student Loan Program, which consisted of matching grants from federal and provincial governments.

7

Tuition was much cheaper in those days–average national tuition in 1951, for example, was only $230 per year–and after the Second World War there had even been talk of scrapping tuition fees altogether. Although education came under provincial jurisdiction, the federal government accounted for a significant share of financial contributions, particularly after the 1951 report of the Royal Commission on National Development in the Arts, Letters and Sciences, chaired by Vincent Massey, which urged federal "patronage" for students at both undergraduate and graduate levels.

The prevailing belief was that post-secondary education should be dictated by students' ability and desire, not their financial means, with government providing the bulk of support for college and university budgets. As late as 1978, government funds accounted for 83.8 per cent of university operating revenue.[8]

In 1964, as part of a general upsurge in investment in education, Lester Pearson's Liberal government created the Canada Student Loans Program, to supplement students' private resources. Loans were provided to qualified students by banks and other financial institutions, which administered the repayment process. These loans were in turn backed by the federal government, which reimbursed lenders in full for any loans that went into default. The arrangement was, obviously, a bonanza for lenders, who had no-risk access to a burgeoning market.

Throughout the 1960s, 70s and early 1980s, post-secondary education expanded steadily.

Things began to change in 1986, when Brian Mulroney's Conservative government limited cash transfers to the provinces for post-secondary schooling to growth in the national economy, minus two per cent. More cash transfer cuts were made in 1989, and in 1991 funding for Established Programs Financing was frozen altogether. Under Jean Chretien's Liberals things continued to spiral downward. In 1995, the Student Financial Assistance Act was passed, ending the full federal guaranty to banks for loan defaults, and substituting instead a so-called "risk share" fee of five per cent payable to banks as compensation for loan losses. The next year, 1996, then-Finance Minister Paul Martin grouped all federal cash transfers for post-secondary education, health and social services into a single Canada Health and Social Transfer--and cut the total amount by $7 billion. The federal cutback was accompanied by decreased funding from many provincial governments, as well.

Tuition fees mushroomed. Between 1985, the year before Mulroney changed the transfer formula, and Martin's 1996 slashing of transfer funds, average annual university tuition had already more than doubled, from $1,019 to $2,384. After Martin's transfer cuts, they more than doubled again, to nearly $5,000 by 2010. As of the 2010-11 school year, the national average was $5,138 per year.

Students and their families had to make up the difference. The government grants of yore were largely history, replaced by loans, and with the rises in tuition, relief in the form of private foundation scholarships was barely a drop in the bucket. Students who weren't from wealthy families had no choice but to cover the gap by taking on debt.

The loan system was on its way..... toward monsterhood.

Road to ruin

"How do I love thee?" sang the poet. "Let me count the ways.[9]"

"How do I ruin thee?" today's student loan system seems to mock. And, in roughly ascending order of destructiveness, here are some of the ways Canada's present method of financing post-secondary education is ruining young people and the country. Our system, much like its U.S. counterpart:

1) prices post-secondary education, at both community college and university levels, out of the reach of an increasing number of high school graduates;
2) discourages those who earn community college diplomas from going on to university programs;
3) discourages university graduates with bachelor's degrees from going on to graduate school for a masters or doctorate. In some cases, honors graduates who might have contributed uniquely valuable research have dropped out of further education and gone to work at minimum wage jobs, rather than continue to accumulate more debt. Sociologists call this "debt aversion;" and agree it makes sense when a typical bachelor's graduate already owes $18,000 to $25,000 on leaving school;
4) prices medical school out of the reach of many students from low-income or middle class families, skewing the profile of med-school entrants in favor of the wealthy;
5) saddles medical school graduates who are not from wealthy families with average debts of $250,000 or more;
6) encourages medical graduates to practice in affluent urban areas, rather than poorer rural or inner-city areas, so as to earn more money and pay off their loan debts more quickly;

7) encourages medical graduates to avoid family medicine and opt instead for more lucrative medical specialties, so as to pay off loan debts more quickly;
8) encourages some medical graduates to emigrate to the U.S., where the for-profit health systems in some states may yield higher salaries, with which to pay off student loan debts;
9) prices law school out of reach of many students from low-income or middle class families, skewing the profile of law school entrants in favor of the wealthy;
10) encourages law graduates to practice in affluent urban areas, rather than in rural or inner-city areas, so as to earn more money to pay off student loans;
11) discourages law graduates from doing *pro bono* (free, "for the public good") work, such as taking on some class action suits or doing Legal Aid work;
12) encourages law graduates to specialize in more lucrative corporate or business law, rather than other specialties like environmental law, so as to pay student loans more quickly;
13) forces students with physical or mental disabilities to pay significantly more for their education than non-disabled students. A deaf student, for example, may pay up to $60,000 more for a bachelor's degree than his or her non-deaf counterpart;
14) prevents disabled students from attending post-secondary schools set up specifically to accommodate their disabilities. In some cases,

enrolment in such specialty schools has dropped by 70 per cent or more;
15) through "capping" limits on maximum borrowing periods or amounts, interrupts students and cuts off their loans before they have completed a degree. Students working towards masters or doctoral degrees are especially vulnerable. Their studies can be halted and loan payments and interest become due before they can finish their work;
16) leads to the gouging of foreign students who wish to study in Canada, treating them as "cash cows." This violates the 1976 International Covenant on Economic, Social and cultural Rights, to which treaty Canada is a signatory;
17) hobbles college and university graduates with heavy debt for years after graduation, preventing them from making other economy-stimulating investments, such as buying homes or autos, as well as from marrying and starting families;
18) tends to encourage students–particularly medical and law school students--to take on more loans than they really need, thus increasing their post-graduation period of indebtedness. Banks often hard-sell such "preferred" students to take on "generous" lines of credit over and above their government loans;
19) is a needlessly complex system, rife with confusion, incompetence, invasion of privacy and fraud. In many cases, borrowers cannot even find out how much they owe, what the interest is on their outstanding balance, what their monthly payments are or how many years it will take to pay

off their loan. When figures are given, they often change without explanation, and no evidence is provided as to the accuracy of the amounts;
20) saddles graduates who miss payments, or make late payments, with draconian penalties, fees, collection charges and accrued compound interest, sometimes totaling more than the original loan itself and creating a *de facto* tax on the working poor;
21) often forces students–even including some who have **not** missed or been late for any loan payments–into default, resulting in their being ruthlessly hounded by collection agencies;
22) has given rise to a mass of collection agency abuses, including illegal actions, harassment and abuse of third parties (families, neighbors, co-workers or employers of graduates);
23) has given rise to fears that Canada may adopt the U.S. practice of jailing graduates who cannot make student loan payments[10], reviving the supposedly long-dead concept of debtors' prisons ("Are there no prisons? And the union workhouses, are they still in operation?" railed Dickens' Ebenezer Scrooge[11]);
24) put much student lending into the hands of companies, or their subsidiaries, with shocking histories of public scandal and law breaking, on both sides of the Canada/U.S. border;
25) caused the federal government, since 2000, to assign collection of loan defaults to the Canada Revenue Agency, rather than private collectors. The agency, however, recruits personnel from the

same private collection companies it has replaced, personnel whose biases and methods of work may remain after they've changed jobs;
26) has made students and graduates into a new class of citizen, shorn of a basic right enjoyed by all other Canadians. While others, should they fall upon hard times due to sickness, unemployment or family emergency, may clear their debts by declaring bankruptcy, students cannot. Alone among the population, holders of student debts are forbidden to discharge them in bankruptcy for at least seven years after graduation. Many see this as a violation of the Canadian Charter of Rights, while pointing out the irony that badly-managed collection agencies that fall on hard times may declare bankruptcy, but their targets cannot;
27) has led to potential conflicts of interest, where university employees and administrators have contacts or business relationships with companies that provide loans, or with collection agencies. Some schools distribute preferred lender lists to students, naming particular companies. In one case, a university president and board member was also an executive employed by a private loan company;
28) starves university researchers of funds to carry on their work, while simultaneously weeding out many promising students who may have become brilliant researchers;
29) encourages a mindset among university administrators that favors a "pro-business," model, putting profit above academic freedom and

diversity, and discouraging the idea of education as a human right, rather than a commodity for sale;
30) encourages universities to invest in narrowly business-related or technology-related disciplines, rather than in the arts or in pure research disciplines;
31) makes colleges and universities more dependent on donations from private industry, which often come with strings attached;
32) discourages the original goal of university education, namely to develop graduates with the ability to think independently, creatively and critically;
33) encourages the development of timid, reluctant graduates, more preoccupied with keeping a job, so as to pay off loans, than in contributing to society;
34) creates, via privatization, a non-accountable kind of "shadow government," not subject to regulations that bind the regular civil service, which eventually spreads to many other phases of the bureaucracy, not only education. One privately owned student loan service provider, for example, has also taken over the production of a provincial government's publications, as well as much of the administration of the controversial federal long-gun registry;
35) prevents young people from reaching their full professional earnings potential, thus assuring that they will contribute less to society in terms of lifetime taxes;

36) assures higher unemployment and underemployment rates, by preventing young people from obtaining optimal training for jobs;
37) damages the physical and mental/emotional health of students and graduates, sometimes severely;
38) drives students and graduates with heavy debts into illegal and dangerous activity, to earn money to pay off loans. These activities may include prostitution, gambling, involvement in the drug trade, and taking part in risky medical trials;
39) drives many students to contemplate suicide, and has driven several, in both the U.S. and Canada, to actually kill themselves.

This is only a partial list.

Of course, no system developed by humans is all bad. On the plus side, our way of financing post-secondary education:

1) has increased the profits of several banks, finance agencies, and especially collection agencies, while providing jobs for their staffs, which may number in the hundreds;
2) has given politicians an excuse to claim that their programs are generously "aiding" students (imagine applying the title "auto aid" to the granting of automobile loans with similar terms of credit);
3) has swollen the election campaign coffers of some political parties and politicians;
4) has, in the words of one student wag, enabled neoconservative ideologues to "realize their wet dreams" by privatizing government.

Life is a trade-off.
But don't take my word for this tale of woes. Listen to what the students have to say.

1. Canadian Association of University Teachers, *CAUT Almanac of Post-Secondary Education in Canada 2011-2012* (Ottawa: 2012), 25.

2. Canadian Federation of Students, *Public Education for the Public Good* (Ottawa: 2011), 14.

3. *Ibid.*, 15.

4. Superintendent of Financial Institutions in Canada, Office of the Chief Actuary, *Actuarial Report on the Canada Student Loans Program, as at 31 July 2009* (Ottawa: Office of the Chief Actuary, 2009), 22.

5. Joseph Berger, Anne Motte and Andrew Parkin, *The Price of Knowledge: Access and Student Finance in Canada*, Canada Millenium Scholarship Foundation (Montreal: 2007), 129.

6. Coalition for Student Loan Fairness, *"Canadian student loan interest is more than double charged by most countries,"* 5 July 2007, as posted online at: http://www.bankruptcycanada.com/blog/category/canadian-student-loans/

7. *Ibid.*

8. Statistics Canada, *Government Funding and Tuition as a Share of University Operating Revenue*, 1978-2008, as posted on Worthwhile Canadian Initiative: A mainly Canadian economics blog, 12 December 2011, http://worthwhile.typepad.com/worthwhile_canadian_initi/2011/02/ca...

9. Elizabeth Barrett Browning, "To George Sand: a desire."

10. Imprisonment for debt was abolished federally in the U.S. in 1833, and most states outlawed it in the 1850s. However, following pressure from the credit industry, the practice has been revived, and more than a third of U.S. states currently allow borrowers–including holders of student loans--to be jailed for non-payment of debts. See: *Debtors' Prison* - Wikipedia http://en.wikipedia.org/wiki/Debtors'_prison

11. Charles Dickens, *A Christmas Carol* (Mineola, N.Y.: Dover Publications Inc., 1991), 5-6.

Chapter Two: "You reach a number, and you're out...."

"My ships have all miscarried, my creditors grow cruel...."

-- W. Shakespeare, *The Merchant of Venice*

The most important thing about Nereid Lake's story is that it's not unusual. She's just good at telling it, at expressing herself. She has a gift for language, after all.

"I was part way through a master's degree in French linguistics at Simon Fraser University," she said. "The Canadian Linguistics Association had accepted the very first paper which I wrote at the master's level, for international publication. My aspiration was to work in the field of voice recognition cognitive science, getting computers to understand human language. I was a high academic achiever, actually making a splash in the world of linguistics. I had an armload of awards. I won awards every year. I was scheduled to present [the paper] at Simon Fraser, and again in Toronto.

"Then Canada Student Loans basically threw me out. They said: You've reached your lifetime lending limit. Get out of school. 'Lifetime lending limit,' I remembered those words because they're so alliterative.

"I was born to a poor family, a family where I was the only university graduate. My parents split up when I was nine, after their business failed, and I was raised by a single mom. There just wasn't money for school. I thought Student Loans was going to be the Great Equalizer. But they said leave.

"So I left school.

"I really wanted to work in voice recognition technology. I do feel I had something to contribute. I was able to detect syntactical structure in languages that nobody else had been able to document before.

"Words convey meaning. How do they do that? Why are verbs verbs? What do they contain in them that makes them indicative of a state or an action? That kind of underlying structure gets mapped out [by linguists] in things called syntactic trees. I had pointed out in one of my papers that the imperative in French, and likewise in English and any language that has an imperative, has an element of time. It had been assumed in the previous literature that time was not one of the branches of the syntactic tree of an imperative.

"I actually demonstrated that it was.

"But Canada Student Loans said no, get out. It's not relevant how well you're achieving, or what you might have to contribute, or if you're in a field where Canada doesn't have enough people. You reach a number and you're gone."

Six months after a student leaves school, whether employed or not, he or she is expected to start repaying the loans. At the time she was forced out, Ms. Lake owed approximately $60,000, on which interest was charged at eight per cent.

Since she hadn't finished her master's, she was unable to get work in her chosen field of linguistics. On top of that, she found that many places that pay well won't hire anyone who has student loan debts outstanding. "I've had job interviews where they want to know if you have student loan debt," she said. "If you do, you're not in. One was with the Canadian government, in tourism, and the other was in law enforcement. They don't want you if you owe money.

"I found a job as a court clerk, making about $2,300 a month, net" she said, "a position for which far less education than mine is normally sufficient qualification." She took the job partly because few others were accessible to someone with a loan debt, and partly because "my loans are both federal and provincial, and the province of British Columbia, for whom I work, had a program that knocks a certain amount off my provincial loan debt each year that I remain an employee."

At that point, no longer in school but at least gainfully employed, she entered a world known only to student borrowers, a kind of Neverland, where nothing to do with their loans ever makes sense again, where it's never possible to get straight answers, and where, it seems, one's debt can never actually be repaid.

A timeline

Ms. Lake lives in Vancouver, where the cost of living is high and the price of housing still higher. In fact, the city is the world's second-least affordable place to find a home, according to a recent Demographia International Housing Affordability Survey.[1] With a median housing price of $678,500 and median income of $63,800, it is second only to Hong Kong in cost.

"I have a daughter," she explained. "I have a husband [not her daughter's biological father] whose business is failing, but he can't get out of it quite yet because he's got contracts to fulfill. His income is negative, so I have two dependents. We live in a housing cooperative, this very humble place that has leaky co-op syndrome, and we pay almost $1,000 a month in rent. We live well below the Canadian poverty line, because more than 40 per cent of my income goes just to shelter. They set the poverty line at where you are spending more than 40 per cent of your income on basics like food, clothing and shelter, and I spend more than 40 per cent on shelter alone. I don't know what we'd do if I was forced to seek market housing. Live in a car?" When the Student Loan system assessed her a monthly payment that was beyond her financial ability to provide–nearly $500–a struggle began that has continued for several years. At first her focus was only on the day-to-day battle, but eventually Ms. Lake began doing something most graduates don't do. She started to keep careful track of what was happening to her, in the form of a timeline.

It makes for a long list, which takes patience to read through, but it took more patience to live through. The stories of hundreds, perhaps thousands of students, could match, or in terms of hardship and outrage, far surpass it:

My Canada Student Loans [see endnote][2] Timeline – Nereid Lake (originally prepared 04 March 2011)

<u>NOTE:</u> First as a single parent (truly single: my child's only parent: no child support), and then as the sole wage-earner in a family of 3, my government-clerk's income has always been so low as to make repayment of my student loans unfeasible. For many years, I did not keep careful records, because I had faith that my government would treat me fairly and sensibly. Was I ever wrong!

<u>August 2006:</u> I reach the 6-months-out-of-school milestone and am assessed an "affordable" payment of nearly $500 per month (keep in mind that *I'm a single parent taking home about $2,300.00 per month)*. Some student loan payments are taken directly from my bank account without my consent, causing me to miss a payment of my housing charge (rent). I switch banks to prevent this from happening again.

<u>November 2006:</u> After months of jumping through red-tape hoops, I am placed on *Interest Relief*, backdated to 01

October 2006. No payments are required of me now. Despite the fact that Student Loans recognizes that my income has always been too low to permit repayment, they will not return the payments they have taken from me. There is no ombudsman. It takes months for me to recover from the financial blow of the August withdrawals.

Many cycles of *Interest Relief* go by, and at nearly every cusp, the following events happen: **(1)** I am required to reapply, and told that I should not supply proof of income for my reapplication. **(2)** My application is rejected because I did not supply proof of income; I am assessed an unreasonable payment. **(3)** Bank R [third-party lender bank] then demands payment on the portion of my loans which it holds. **(4)** Upset and frightened, I re-submit my application to Canada Student Loans, this time including the proof of income I was told not to provide before. **(5)** My application is accepted and back-dated to join up with the end of my previous cycle of *Interest Relief*. **(6)** Bank R backs off and all is well again. Aside from the inefficiency and stress of this repetitive little drama, my relationship with Student Loans and the *Interest Relief* program is largely unproblematic.

February 2009: Due to budgetary restrictions in the Provincial Government (my employer), my First Aid Certificate is not renewed. The fact that I no longer act as a staff first-aider takes $50.00 off of each paycheque I receive: *my average income goes down to $2,200.00 per month.* Coincidentally, my housing co-op raises its housing charge at this same time to pay for its leaky-co-op syndrome and mould problems.

August 2009: My long-time self-employed boyfriend's small business is faltering and he is behind in his rent; he can't afford to keep going, so I offer to take him on as a dependent. We enter a common-law relationship with me as the household income-earner. Now *three* people are living on $2,200.00 per month.

September 2009: The *Interest Relief* program is cancelled without warning. I am informed that I may apply for the *Repayment Assistance* program. This new program[3] has a built-in one-day period of non-overlap with the previous program cycle. The gap of one day puts every student borrower out of good standing, and we are all required to pay interest on at least that day before our new applications will be processed. It's only $7.29 for me, but the principle of the thing bothers me: they have designed it for incomprehensibility, delay, inconvenience, fear and frustration. After paying the $7.29, I am placed on *Repayment Assistance* and assessed a monthly payment of $0.

April 2010: I reapply for *Repayment Assistance*, but my application is rejected for unspecified reasons. The letter I receive on 20 April 2010 just says they "cannot process" my application. I call their call-centre (which is a private debt-collection agency) and write them multiple letters and re-submit my *Repayment Assistance* application.

June 2010: I receive a letter (dated 09 June 2010) saying that I may have my *Repayment Assistance* reinstated, but only if I first pay $291.35 "to bring your loan up to date." What does that even mean? The call-centre employees I spoke to did not know: it was just a number on their computer screen. When I escalated the matter to the call-centre supervisors, they also had access only to what was on their computer screens, so I asked to speak to a manager. The manager said that I had to keep in mind that they were just a private collection agency, and that they would only know what the Canada Student Loans Service Centre gave them to know; that if I wanted information on my actual loan, or insight into why any payment was assessed to me, I would have to take it up with Student Loans. But there's no way to phone Student Loans directly: the only phone contact is the call centre. I could fax them, but I would have to wait to receive any answer by post. There is no ombudsman.

July 2010: It was a hardship, but by trimming off of my family's food budget and delaying some utilities payments, I made the arbitrary $291.35 payment and was placed back on *Repayment Assistance*. But now, for some reason, <u>I was assessed a monthly payment amount of over two hundred dollars to Bank R</u>. I write letters and phone the useless call centre, and eventually get assessed a monthly payment of $116.66, to be paid directly to Canada Student Loans. Bank R backs off again. I take my vehicle off the road and allocate what had been the insurance money to pay the $116.66 per month.

In frustration, I withdraw my consent to communicate with Student Loans through the private collection agency they use as their call centre. I invite Student Loans to communicate with me via email or fax, and get no response. There is no ombudsman.

December 2010: I reapply for *Repayment Assistance*, but my application is rejected, and no explanation is given. I am calculated what Canada Student Loans calls an "affordable" monthly payment of $473.49, a little over 20% of what my family of three has to live on each month. I write to Canada Student Loans, offering proof of my common-law husband's meagre income from his small business (which he will probably have to abandon) and official pay notices from my employer.

January 2011: On 25 January 2011, I receive a letter from Canada Student Loans (dated 12 January 2011) saying they were unable to process my latest application because they needed more specific information from me. The very next day, 26 January 2011, I fax them all the documents they requested, along with a plea for instantaneous, electronic, two-way communication.

February 2011: On 03 February 2011, I receive a letter from Canada Student Loans (dated 17 January 2011 – that's right, *five days* after the first one, while the first one was *still in the post*) telling me that it was too late to respond to the request in the first letter: I had left it too long and my application for *Repayment Assistance* had expired. I write to Student Loans, telling them I think it's illegal for them to send a demand via the postal service and then set me up to fail by telling me it's too late to comply with it while it's still in the mail on its way to me. I write to my MP, the Minister of Human Resources and Skills Development, the Minister of Finance, the Ethics Commissioner and the shadow ministers for each of those positions. I re-send my entire *Repayment Assistance* application, including all information about my family's income that I can lay my hands on. On 28 February 2011, I receive a letter from Student Loans saying that I am now on *Repayment Assistance* again, retroactive to 01 December 2010; my payment amount has gone down to zero again, which <u>makes me wonder why, given that my financial picture had not changed since August of 2009, I had ever been assessed any monthly payment at all</u>!

March 2011: On 02 March 2011, I receive a letter from Bank R (dated 17 February 2011) saying that they acknowledged my *Repayment Assistance* status as it was communicated to them [and I note that it was communicated to them via some nearly-instant electronic means, not the postal service], but that they can't process my new status unless I pay them $739.23 in "interest" first. This is not a question of hardship: it's a straight-up impossibility. If I had the kind of finances which would permit me to disburse over seven hundred dollars on demand, I wouldn't need to be on *Repayment Assistance*, would I? This is not just an unreasonable and inhumane demand, it seems calculated to force me into default (which would make me ineligible for further assistance programs). I send letters to both Student Loans and Bank R, but I don't hear back right away.

March 2011: Desperate, I contact the *Canadian Federation of Students* (CFS) to see if there's any help with this situation. My local representative, Ian Boyko, puts me in contact with the *Federation's* president, David Molenhuis. I sign authorizations for Mr Molenhuis and the CFS to act as my agent.

March 2011: I receive a statement from Bank R stating that my outstanding loan with that bank is $0 and that my monthly payment is also $0. This statement arrives with a letter requesting that I destroy (not simply disregard) the previous statement, which states that I owe more than $26,000.00 I take this as confirmation that my student loans were in fact consolidated back in 2006 and that Bank R not only acknowledges that I am not required to make payments to them, but that their past years of demands were both unwarranted and unconscionable (hence the destruction request).

April 2011: Mr Molenhuis meets with representatives from Student Loans, who apparently agree that a seven-hundred-dollar-plus payment is unwarranted. That payment is no longer required, and I am back on Repayment Assistance, with a $0 per month payment. However, Student Loans continues to cash the post-dated cheques I had written, and mysteriously my balance at Bank R doesn't seem to be $0 after all, but nobody can say why.

April 2011: Student Loans sends me a letter stating that they were "unable to process" my application for *Repayment Assistance*. I asked Mr Molenhuis to intervene again, and I finally receive a *Confirmation of Approval* on 17 May 2011 (dated 10 May 2011). Mr Molenhuis requests a detailed accounting of precisely what I owe to whom, including a history of consolidations of my loans, but does not receive it.

May 2011: I give an interview to the *National Post* newspaper, outlining the difficulties I have had staying out of default in an inhumane *Repayment Assistance* system seemingly designed to provoke default. At about this time, I receive a fairly long and difficult-to-follow letter from a Student Loans issue-resolution consultant named Bonnie; I don't understand what it was trying to say, so I forward a copy to Mr Molenhuis.

Mid-May 2011: Mr Molenhuis has a case meeting with Student Loans. Student Loans agrees to repay the amount they had cashed in post-dated cheques during a time when they were not entitled to payments, and also to place me on "Stage 2" Repayment Assistance for 5 years at $0 per month.

June 2011: I receive a cheque from Student Loans equivalent to the amount of two of the post-dated cheques, but I never receive the notification of my "Stage 2" Repayment Assistance status.

June 2011: The *National Post* article is published, but misses the point on the inhumane and incomprehensible system of *Repayment Assistance* which appears designed to force persons in financial difficulty (like me) into default so they can be disqualified from further assistance. The *National Post* article focuses instead on a generation of Canadians (again like me) who were forced to take out loans in order to acquire the basic minimum education needed to participate positively in society and the economy, but who actually find themselves in a worse personal financial situation than if they had foregone education altogether and just worked at McDonalds.

July 2011: In the middle of my current term of *Repayment Assistance* – I receive a form letter telling me that my "application for repayment assistance has expired..." and giving the two reasons that (1) they made a request to Bank R that that bank had failed to respond to, and (2) they had requested information that I had failed to provide. Up until this point, the flow of information between Bank R and Student Loans has appeared to be cordial, abundant and nearly instantaneous; whatever is getting in the way there can't possibly be my fault. And I am almost a hyper-compliant client, frequently providing applications and information about my income "too early"; I have never neglected to provide requested documentation – ever. I fax letters to Student Loans to ascertain the nature of the problem and receive no response.

August 2011: Believing that my current term of *Repayment Assistance* will expire on 01 September 2011, I submit a new application, complete with pay stubs for the month of August 2011. At about this time, I also call Bonnie (this is the first and only time we have ever spoken, despite a claim apparently made to Mr Molenhuis that she and I have had "phone discussions" before). She tells me that my current term ends at the end of September (I have reapplied too early again), but that she foresees my next application being rejected anyway because she thinks that Bank R is calculating me an outstanding amount owing of "around $400". I have no letter or other documentation from Bank R stating such a thing. I asked Bonnie why I wasn't on "Stage 2" Repayment Assistance after the deal struck in May, and she responds that Mr Molenhuis must have been "mistaken" about the arrangement.

September 2011: I call Bonnie a second time to discuss the "around $400" and ask *why, 66 months into repayment, I suddenly have to make a payment directly to Bank R (having never paid them any amount before)*. Bonnie is away on vacation, so I speak to a person who identifies herself as

"Shirley". Shirley tells me that she thinks the "around $400" calculated as being in default has to do with a program gap: apparently Bank R had a program in place that tracked my *Repayment Assistance* status, but that program quietly ended and another one started, and in the interregnum I was thrown into default without being informed. In that very same conversation with Shirley, I learned that the organization I have been dealing with for 66 months, the *National Student Loans Service Centre*, is not a branch of the federal government after all, but yet another private corporation. I don't even know the last time I dealt with an actual public servant with regard to my student loans.

September 2011: Despite other areas of my life going well (healthy, scholastically-successful child; great relationship with my husband; reasonable home life; a job that doesn't pay too well, but which I enjoy), the stress of my financial situation (especially student loans) is affecting my health. As a BC government employee, I am entitled to free mental health care, and I sign up for stress counselling.

Lake's timeline ended there, but not for long. In later e-mail communications to Molenhuis, she added to it:

29 November 2011: Remember how Student Loans Issue Resolutions Analyst Bonnie offered to process my Repayment Assistance application, how she then sent a letter telling me she had closed my account with her office two days after I had faxed my application, and hasn't taken a single call from me since? Well, I managed to navigate their phone tree to talk to a couple of Bonnie's coworkers, once on 3 November, the day I received the letter about closing my account, and once a week after, because I hadn't heard back. During each call, I was told my application needed confirmation of my family size. During each conversation I provided it, and was told the application would now proceed. Today I received a letter from "Borrower Services," informing me that I am one payment past due and my total past due amount is $306. Past due? I'm supposed to be on Repayment Assistance, with no payment due, and had the assurance of three different people at the Issue Resolution office that it would be taken care of. I never received any notification about my Repayment status, even when I asked. Whenever I called Bonnie's office, I got either a voice notification of her unavailability, which did not permit me to leave a message, or yet another request for my family size, or assurance from one of her coworkers that my application was being processed. I never received notification that I was in non-Repayment Assistance status and that my monthly payment had been reassessed at $306.

My husband is still looking for a job, ever more desperately; he is now attempting to parlay his Vancouver Olympics experience into a job with London Olympics, just to obtain any sort of job at all. Needless to say, with three people living on my $2,200 a month in Vancouver, there isn't anything like $306 a month available. I'm the kind of Canadian the Repayment Assistance Program purports to help; instead I just feel victimized. It's tempting to think that the Issue Resolution office exists only to lull student borrowers facing hard financial times into a false sense of security, so that they go into default. Do you have any advice on how to proceed?

14 December 2011: Well, it doesn't slow down, even for the holidays. I've received a form letter saying that Student

Loans can't process my application until I call their phone centre. As you know, I do not consent (and haven't for years) to working with their phone centres for two reasons: 1) nobody there has any insight or authority to actually negotiate with me, or address real issues pertaining to my account, but 2) and equally important, my history with them shows that when you talk to their phone centres the conclusions reached depend on the employee you happened to talk to, and you end up with no documented evidence of the understanding reached. So the next time you call, the picture is totally different, and nobody can explain why.

I've even been quoted an amount to "put my account back in good standing," and when I called back later the same day was told the amount was $150 more than the first quote! They couldn't explain the discrepancy at all. Have you any advice on how I can compel Student Loans to deal with me on paper, so every arrangement is properly documented?

And finally, one last, long lament:

15 December 2011: I thought you'd like to see the next round. It should be a grim sort of diversion if nothing else. When I received notification that I was already a month behind on the $306 payments, which I had not even been informed were assessed to me, I sent the National Student Loan Service Centre a seven-page fax, comprising an explanatory letter, the original fax I'd sent their Issue Resolution analyst who had left me in the lurch, and a request that my Repayment Assistance application be processed as if it had been received on or before the date I faxed it to Issue Resolutions. Then yesterday I received a form letter saying my application couldn't be processed until I provided more information to their phone centre.

Now, a human wouldn't send that letter, because it must be plastered all over my file that I do not consent to conducting business verbally with their phone centre employees. Not only do they not have the insight or authority for our interaction to be meaningful, but the understanding reached appears to depend on which employee happens to take your call, and you are left with no documentation. Therefore any understanding reached is at best ephemeral and at worst illusory.

I responded the same day via fax, which is instantaneous. My letter reminded them that I have no confidence in their call centre's ability to conduct bona fide business and make enforceable arrangements, and chided them gently about the vagueness of their request for information. I could have provided the very information they purported to seek in the same fax transmission. Instead, I expect to hear back via post in two weeks or so, by which time I have no doubt my application will have "expired."

sigh

In that same fax transmission, I suggested that their continuing stubbornness in communicating with me exclusively by post in the name of "security" was counterproductive, if not downright backwards. I live in Vancouver's Downtown Eastside, in a housing cooperative where the apartment building's mailbox has a history of break-ins. The fax machine at the courthouse where I work is more secure in every way than the post. It appears to me the deciding factor in their chosen mode of communication is in fact delay, not security.

sigh again.

So I have demonstrated that I'm willing to provide any information they require, but I expect to have another event similar to the one in February, when they declared it too late for me to comply even while their demand letter was still in the mail. I am documenting every exchange. There will definitely be something to set before the judge.......

Hoping that the darkness of winter is lightened and warmed for you by whatever stripe of holiday rings your bell.

The saga continued, and as it did became more and more outrageous, culminating in the bank apparently ignoring all previous agreements and discussions, even with the Canadian Federation of Students, and abruptly sending Lake's file to a collection agency.

18 January 2012: Can you please get back to me soon with information on what has been done every other time Bank R has made impossible demands for lump-sum payments? This time it's $542.16 they are demanding. Please read the attached scan of the letter I received this morning, and see if you don't interpret it as I do: "Give us $542.16 or we will get you kicked off Repayment Assistance." It actually seems a little like extortion, when interpreted in this fashion.

Bank R, knowing as they do that the reason I'm on Repayment Assistance is because there's nothing of my income left over to make loan payments, has to have some strategy in mind when demanding lump-sums of this magnitude. Do you know what that is? It' sort of appears that they are trying to FINE me for having a low income and availing myself of relief programs.

And, as I've said above, I am very anxious to know what steps you and/or Jeffrey (sp?) took to get Bank R to abandon their demand in previous instances of this kind: they have demanded up to over $700 in the past, and you seemed to have some method of getting them to behave rationally; I need that kind of help again.

Thanks for your quick response, with thanks (and a great deal of anxiety),

Nereid

27 January 2012: I wrote to you on January 18th, just 9 days ago, attaching a scan of a letter from Bank R (on Bank R letterhead) demanding that I pay $542.16 in "arrears." The questions on my mind at that time were:

1. How can someone go into "arrears" with with a $0/month payment?

2. Is Bank R allowed to just make up its own rules and assign arbitrary (and impossible) lump-sum payments when I'm on RAP?

These were questions you were going to get sorted out when Canada Student Loans gave you the full statement of my account that you requested.

Well, today I am in receipt of another Bank R demand letter (this time on Agency A Collections letterhead). Today's letter is demanding immediate payment of $23,514.81, which is not merely inhumane but also ludicrous: I'm on Repayment Assistance, with a monthly payment of $0 because my income is that low. I don't even have the five-hundred-odd bucks they arbitrarily demanded on the 18th; how is it that they think I'd have the means to make a disbursement of tens of thousands of dollars?

And how can they act thusly (demanding these tens of thousands of dollars) when we haven't even sorted out the issues of loan consolidation and arbitrary assignments of hundreds of dollars in "arrears" despite my RAP status? Honestly, I am still not convinced that the Annual Statement they sent me on 21 January 2011 (saying I owed Bank R $0.00 and asking me to destroy documents from them that claimed otherwise) did not constitute an admission that my 2006 loan consolidation meant that they were not entitled to any payments from me. Now I've got this demand for an even-more-impossible lump-sum payment. I've got a grand total of $19.91 in my savings account, and my chequing account is regularly overdrawn. That's why I'm on RAP to begin with: my income is not really adequate for my family's needs (and we live pretty modestly in a housing co-op in Vancouver's worst neighbourhood).

I've been trying to cultivate a calmness around all this student loans nightmare (it's not easy, but knowing you're on my team helps); it's really hard not to feel stressed out about this latest blow.

Feeling awfully bullied, and hoping you have good news (or at least words of comfort and advice),

Nereid

The feeling Lake expressed in her 29 November entry, that the system was actually trying to push borrowers into default, may not be as wild a speculation as she thought. As later chapters will describe, there is evidence that, particularly in the

U.S. but perhaps also in Canada, forcing borrowers into default could be a deliberate strategy. An article by Alan Collinge in the *New York Times*, commenting on the American situation, explained:

> "Simple averaging suggests that overall, about one in three student borrowers are defaulting on their student loans....... In 2004, the Department of Education predicted that it would get back every dollar of principal, plus almost 20 per cent in interest and fees for defaulted loans. Combined with the fact that the dominant lenders in the student loan market like Sallie Mae own collection companies that make tremendous amounts of money from the collection of defaulted loans, one can see both wouldn't be overly excited at the prospect of the public knowing that the student loan default rate was higher than that for credit cards, payday loans, sub-prime mortgages, or any other type of loan in existence.

> "This mindset has led to horrible oversight of the student loan program. Instead of working hard to keep the default rates down by pressuring universities to provide a good product at a low price, exactly the opposite has occurred. The Department of Education has no interest in a low default rate.... How can the Department of Education be making money on defaulted loans instead of losing money? Simple. Congress removed nearly every consumer protection from these loan instruments, including standard bankruptcy protections, statutes of limitations, truth in lending requirements, and others. In addition, Congress gave the department and its lenders draconian collection powers to, frankly, extort not just the original principal and interest from the borrowers, but also a massive amount in penalty fees and collection costs. This leads to an environment where students are often defaulted, despite

their efforts to keep their loans in good stead, allowing the lenders to tack on massive penalties that stick.

It is really quite amazing how much free money can be made in the absence of bankruptcy protections, and the Department of Education is a willing player in the game. Of course, given that the Office of Federal Student Aid is run largely by former executives of student loan companies like Sallie Mae, it is understandable how one of our public agencies could be turned into a willing participant in a predatory lending scheme."[4]

Of course, the author was describing the U.S. scene. Whether or not this is the case in Canada as well, and thus Ms. Lake has actually been set up to fail, is another question.

There is no doubt, however, that at the time of her last memo to Molenhuis, the system had already forced Lake: a) to leave school before completing her degree; b) to take a clerical job below her level of education; c) to become entangled in a seemingly endless morass of bureaucratic mixups and contradictions and, d) to suffer so much stress that she had to seek counseling.

It had also deprived Canada–a multicultural nation with two official languages and a host of First Nations and immigrant tongues, all of which need technological accommodation in the age of the Internet--of a promising linguistics specialist whose work might have materially advanced computer science.

Lake is 40 now, no longer the idealistic young undergraduate of the past. "I feel I'm getting too old to go back to school and pick up where I left off," she said. "I don't feel

I'm willing to do this again. This is torture. I love my kid and I value education. I value sharing of information. And I still would tell my daughter not to do student loans."

The experience has made her cynical.

"You can't really get anywhere in the world today with merely a high school education. And that's where this whole caste issue comes in, the feeling of being punished for daring to step outside your caste. The system is saying: 'You were born to a family of humble means; you should be a gas station attendant. You're not supposed to be an award-winning linguist. How dare you try to step outside of that!'

"I think Canada's history of social democracy has been eroded."

As already noted, Lake's story is not unusual, but typical, which is why it has been detailed at length here. Mark O'Meara, who himself has been a student loan borrower, hosts a website called CanadaStudentDebt.ca. On it, he's gathered the testimony of hundreds of borrowers, some with stories similar to Lake's, and some that are much worse..............

1. Steve Ladurantye, "Vancouver among world's 'least affordable' housing markets," *The Globe & Mail*, 23 January 2012, as posted on The Globe & Mail online, http://www.theglobeandmail.com/report-on-business/economy/housing...

2. It turns out Lake had both the name "Canada Student Loans" and the role they played wrong. She was dealing with the National Student Loans Service Centre (NSLSC), which has been administered by private firms working under contract to the government. She notes: "Contrary to what I understood at the time I wrote this outline, they are not a government agency. An employee let that slip during a phone call on September 2011. Until then, I had believed I was dealing with the government." This has been a point of confusion for many students, as will be described in a later chapter.

3. In 2009, in response to complaints from the growing number of students struggling with debt, the federal government created the Canada Student Loan Repayment Assistance Plan. As subsequent chapters will describe, the plan's bureaucratic provisions and the nature of its administration soon came under criticism.

4. Collinge, Alan. "Commentary: A Plea to Add Consumer Protections to Student Loans." *The New York Times*, 11 January 2010, The Choice blog, http://thechoice.blogs.nytimes.com/2010/01/11/bankruptcy/?pagemode...

Chapter Three: Tales from Neverland

"It wearies me, you say it wearies you,
But how I caught it, found it, or came by it,
What stuff 'tis made of, whereof it is born
I am to learn."

—Shakespeare, *The Merchant of Venice*

CanadaStudentDebt.ca is a cacophony of hurt. If it was a musical composition, it's dominant themes would be confusion, chaos and frustration. If it ever reaches a final movement, its climax will come as a crescendo of rage.

But where, exactly to target that rage could be a problem, since the apparent causes of it keep changing names, seemingly changing their own rules, and are about as easy to pin down as a vial of spilled mercury (a later chapter will try to trace a rough history of the firms, agencies and government departments involved). Over the years, since the late 1990s, they've worn the logos of various banks, then their subsidiaries, then a succession of privately-owned entities working under contract to provincial or federal governments, then of those entities' subsidiaries or, alternatively, their parent companies: Unipac, Edulinx, Nelnet, U.S.-based Sallie Mae, First Service, BDP, Repayassist, Tricura, Resolve, D&H Fund, Davis and Henderson. And, of course, National Student Loans Service Centre, Canada Student Loans, Repayment Assistance Plan, Ontario Student Assistance Program (OSAP), and all the other provincial loan programs.

The facade they present to students consists of an army of telephone agents with no last names, no mailing addresses, no easily-contactable supervisors, seemingly no memories and as far as borrowers can tell, a complete inability to think or speak rationally. Students, some of whom may have received loans from up to six different federal, provincial and private sources, leading to a labyrinth of mixups, are left with their heads spinning, and no sympathetic ear.

Except, of course, each other's, which they encounter on Mark O'Meara's godsend of a website. Some of what is said there is mistaken, wrong or the result of mere intemperate venting (O'Meara tries to correct these posts, with webmaster comments, where he can). But some is also, tragically, true. It would be impossible for an objective observer to decide which bits were which, or to contact individual banks or companies to verify details, and thus they are given as-written, with that caveat, and with the private companies and banks designated only by letters of the alphabet. Government departments, supposedly accountable to all Canadians, are named.

Think of these stories as a microphone held out to the chants of protesters--or if you prefer, the shouts of the participants in a riot:

Almost insane

"I almost went insane today, trying to deal with [Company T]–so I was quite relieved to find this website, to see that I'm not the only one who has been subjected to their ridiculous, dead-end, circular arguments," wrote a contributor known as "nectarinee06."

As a matter of policy, the website does not allow contributors to use their real names or addresses, as this has led in the past to students being harassed by spammers, flamers, collection agents or loan consolidation sales staff.

"Below is a letter that I sent to the management at [Company T]," nectarinee06 continued, "but by the sounds of it I suppose it will just be tossed into the mountain high pile of complaints they're likely already dealing with. I don't have the same sympathy for the workers at T as some people may have– everyone needs to earn a living, but there are far less corrupt ways of doing so. As far as I can tell such workers have been specifically trained in how to be confrontational without crossing the line, how to engage in circular arguments, stonewalling, stalling, and being deliberately vague and deceptive. Anyway, I've copied the letter below, and I'm sure many of you will be able to relate to it.

Today I was contacted by your national student loan department and was told that my account was in arrears. I explained that I had previously arranged for automatic debit through your agency to cover arrears from Dec & Jan and to continue with automatic debit on an on-going basis from that point on. I explained that I had done so (on Jan 31/05) by faxing a letter stating the above, as instructed (word for word) by one of your representatives (I have sufficient funds in the bank to cover the debit, so that isn't the issue).

However, the representative who phoned me today could not understand the above. When I suggested that he look at the letter, he said he didn't have it, but someone else in another department did. I asked him to contact that person, but he said he couldn't. I asked if he could contact the person and he said no. I asked to speak to the manager, but he said that wasn't possible. I then asked to speak to the person who originally instructed me to send the letter and he refused to provide me with a name. Instead he insisted on trying to slowly repeat in a patronizing fashion his misunderstanding of the situation.

So I hung up and called back, and again spoke to another representative, who at least said that she would put my call through to the manager. She then said that the manager was busy, and would not be able to contact me for 24 to 72 hours!!!! She would not give me a contact number, nor would she provide any information about any other contacts. So I tried to find this information out for myself by phoning 411, but found that [Company T] is not listed anywhere (sounds like a good investigative newspaper article).

So I called your agency again to find out your fax number, so I that could fax a letter to the manager. The representative told me "no....the manager has to review the file, and then if he thinks it's necessary he will get back to you." I insisted that there must at least be a fax number that I could use to send a letter to the manager, but he said no, there wasn't. When I asked if there was an outside agency that I could complain to, he was not happy with my request and couldn't provide an immediate response, but finally told me to call "O, Canada"???? When I asked if he thought it was odd that clients have absolutely no recourse when they have a problem dealing with his agency, he said "no, this is the way we've always done it." If your staff don't understand what is wrong with the above statement and how it might frustrate some thinking people, then I'm not going to waste my breath explaining it here.

The letter that I faxed on Jan 31/05 is enclosed as is a second letter spelling out again as clearly as I possibly can the fact that I want you to debit my account for all arrears and to continue debiting my account until my loan is paid or I state otherwise.

I would still like to make a complaint about your agency, and in order to do so I would appreciate it if you would provide me with a contact number/address of the chief person in your agency as well as the government agency monitoring your service. You may contact me at [number deleted by webmaster] (please leave a message if I'm not in), or e-mail me at [address deleted]. If you are unable to provide such information, then I would appreciate a short e-mail note to that effect so I can follow-up as necessary.

"Since sending the above letter, I did try again to contact a manager at [Company T] via the 'real' national student loan agency–I didn't punch in my SIN when I called NSL, otherwise they send you directly to [Company T]. I then went to 'alternative means of payment,' and got through to a 'real' NSL representative, who arranged for me to speak to the manager at [Company T]. He assured me that the above problem had been sorted out, but I'll believe it when I see it. I'm also interested to see if they'll actually send me a contact where I can make a complaint.

"Thanks for providing a forum to vent on this very frustrating matter.

"Note: the reason my account was in arrears in the first place is because for some reason the cheques that I sent didn't go through??????? [Company T] has on record that the cheques were received but weren't processed????–although I've never received any notice from my bank. Note there were funds in my account to cover my cheques and I've never received any NSF returned cheques."

Nectarinee06's post sparked several immediate replies:

"These are the biggest group of tools I've ever had the displeasure to talk to," wrote chewsta. "They simply can't get anything right. And everyone there has a different idea of what they want you to do. The best part is that the people you talk to aren't actually in front of your paperwork. No, the people who actually review everything are elsewhere–and can I talk to them? You guessed it."

"Wow! This makes me feel a lot better," added quantummechanic. "Not that I'm happy you all are going through the same shit I am, but it's nice to know that I'm not totally crazy. My story is basically the same as nectarinee06. I've authorized my payments to be debited from my account and no payments have been withdrawn, despite the fact that the money is there.

"But more importantly, here is why I'm glad to see I'm not alone. We have power in numbers and if you are willing to help I'd like to take your problem to the news media. The fact that a government loan is being handled so poorly by a contracted agency and that there is no recourse for those of us who are trying to make our payments honestly, is a genuine news story. Combine that with the potential of a class action lawsuit to cover any extra interest payments, administrative fees to cover late payments due to company fault, and possible damage to personal credit, gives us power to force [Company T] to deal with us honestly and swiftly.

"Every time I speak to this company I get a different story. This reads like a classic scam and I'm willing to raise a stink to make a change. I have been working in film and television for over a decade and am confident I can get someone from at least one major network to look into this. But not if I'm alone. If I'm the only one who will speak up there is no story, and no one will help."

Borrowers like the above, who have been making their payments, or trying to make payments, only to discover that they are nevertheless threatened with being thrown into default, or have actually been put there, are understandably upset. Like Nereid Lake, they start to feel as if lenders are actually trying to force default, rather than go on accepting reasonable, regular payments.

As it turns out, this suspicion may not be as far-fetched and counter-intuitive as it seems. There is considerable evidence, especially from the U.S., that some creditors see default–and the lucrative fees, extra interest and penalties that go with it--as more profitable than simply collecting normal loan payments. A later chapter will go into more detail.

Worse shocks
While it can be a shock to be threatened with default, other borrowers get worse jolts. For example, a poster using the moniker of "nido" wrote, in 2011:

"I'm hoping someone can help me. I went out Christmas shopping Saturday morning and tried to use my debit card and got insufficient funds. I got paid a few days before, so I know the money was there.

"I went to the bank teller and they told me that there was a debit for the exact balance on my account. So here is where it gets fishy. The 'debit' was from '[Company I].' Never heard of it. The message on my account was to call '[Company F].' Never heard of them.

"I have never authorized any type of automatic debits on my account, so I got angry at the teller (for obvious reasons; they just cleaned me out–literally–they never left me five cents), so I demanded to speak to the branch manager. After some digging on his part, he told me that '[Bank C] Collections' authorized the debit. He calls them while I am sitting there.

"This mope proceeds to tell me that it's for a student loan. I lost my freaking mind. As far as I am concerned my student loans are paid off. I paid the government–they took over my [Bank C] loan back when they integrated the student loans.

"Am I missing something? Are they allowed to literally clean out my bank account one week before Christmas? I have two kids. I couldn't go to work this morning because I had no gas in my truck or any money for parking even.

"I have been trying to contact someone from all three of these companies regarding this phantom loan (btw this loan is from 1999)–[Bank C Collections, Company I and F]–and keep getting sent around in circles. Advice?"

Two people replied to this post. First "pvcm:"

"I was told by a government collector that student debt is 100 per cent recoverable, which means they can keep cleaning you out until the debt is paid."

O'Meara himself advised: "Immediately open another bank account at another bank. Change your direct deposit info immediately. Otherwise it will likely happen to your next pay as well."

This for a student loan which the borrower thought had been paid in full years before, but which apparently had been passed down the line at some point to one or more collection agencies. Such agencies, which purchase debts from the original lenders and hope to earn a fee by recovering them, may be unaware that a loan has been paid out, or not care that it has, since they would be after their own fee regardless of whether the original lender was satisfied or not.

Yet more surreal are posts from borrowers who would like some very basic information, such as how much, exactly, they owe. Wrote one of these:

"I have a question related specifically to [Company G] Student Loans Collections. I have one student loan in collections and I had the misfortune of getting these guys. Aside from the multiple usual offences (++calling, abusive agents, refusing payment, not cashing cheques, then cashing them *en masse*, etc.) I seem to have more problems with them now that I'm paying them, than when I was unemployed. I've been paying my loan for over a year now, but I can't seem to get a statement of my account from them. I've requested multiple times. All I get is a letter that says a payment has been made on my account. No amount and no interest rate (which I suppose is better than when they sent me nothing at all). A balance is included but when I've called they've told me the amount is incorrect.

"My payment and amount don't add up and since I can't see what the interest rate is, I have no idea what's being credited to my account. They have given me so many stories that I don't believe anything any of them tell me anymore. I believe I'm entitled to a statement of my account, but how do I force them to send it to me?

"I called [Bank C] (originator of this loan before collections) and told them how I can't get a statement and they told me they would put in a request to [Company G], but I'm not all that hopeful at this point. I asked them what I would have to do to get my loan back to [Bank C] and was told today that it's up to [Company G] to make that decision. Now [Company G's] latest gimmick is to send your call to an answering machine and leave your phone number and they will get back to you. I'm not going to leave my new cell number, so getting a hold of them has been impossible the last two days. I really could use some advice. If I stop paying them, the only one who gets screwed is me."

Contributions to CanadaStudentDebt.ca are grouped under various headings, including News, Announcements and Alerts; Urgent Help Needed; Bankruptcy and Proposal Info and Issues; Privacy Issues, Violations and Complaints; Dealing with Abusive Collection Agencies; Rehabilitating Loans-Getting Out of Collections; Recommended Advocates and Counselors; Credit Repair Information; Small Claims Court; Stress and

Mental Health (which includes Death by Student Loans); and many other topic headings.

There are dozens of stories and replies under each heading, some irritating, some intriguing, some humorous and some outright horrible. Dip into the website anywhere and you will come up with handfuls. For example, a post from Stewart, under the heading "In Exile:"

In exile

"Here's a story that few may have heard of before.

"I graduated with a B.A. in 1988. For close to a year I was unable to find anything more than a part-time job that paid $5 an hour. Taking control of my life (so I thought), I decided to come to Asia to teach English and make big money, and pay off my $18,000 loan [Bank C]. At that time, teaching paid $17 an hour.

"Unfortunately, having just arrived in Asia with no teaching experience meant that, although the per hour salary was good, the number of teaching hours was low. During my first year in Asia I made enough to live, but I saved very little. Therefore, I contacted [Bank C] to request a further (final) six-month extension to delay loan repayment. I was told that because I was abroad that this was impossible, and that repayment of my loan was due immediately. That was money I just didn't have.

"Shortly afterwards a collection agency began to call and harass my parents. The message that was passed on to me was that I risked prosecution and possible jail time. Of course, I knew then, as I know now, that's not possible....probably. So, what was to be a year or two in Asia teaching English has turned into 15 years. I've only ever returned for short visits (a week or two every couple of years). My plan was never to get a free education and then run away, but one year passed into another year as I tried to make enough and save enough to pay off my loan with all the accumulated interest.

"Any advice, anyone? I'm now 40 years old. Should I just accept my fate, or keep hoping to save enough to buy my freedom (with interest, now maybe $50,000) back in Canada?"

One reply noted what was true at that time, but if Canada follows the U.S. lead and revives the ancient concept of debtors' prisons, may not be true in future, namely:

"You can't go to jail for your student loans. The collection agency lied to you and possibly broke the law by contacting your family members. Unfortunately, there is no agency to police the collection agencies......"

Under the topic My Story, ministerofdebt wrote:

"My eyes are sore from reading the student loan act for the last couple of hours before finding this site. Basically, I've been trying to get on interest relief [allowed in certain financial hardship cases] for the last year with the National Student Loan Service Centre. At least that's the company I'm under the assumption that I'm dealing with. Long story short, I owed $19,000 and applied for interest relief. Documents I sent in, including pay stubs, would go missing; documents I faxed in would go missing. People I talked to at the NSLSC would mislead me, including telling me that my interest relief application was being reviewed and I would be contacted shortly. Every time I would speak to someone at the NSLSC I would get a different story. My requests to speak with a supervisor would be met with 'sorry sir,' 'sorry sir.'

"Finally, the letter comes in the mail a month and a half later claiming that they hadn't received my pay stubs for two months (the two pay stubs I had faxed in and had received confirmation that they had been received). Somehow this information was now missing again. Now the runaround began, through the month of December. It seemed, according to NSLSC my student loan was now with another agency in Ontario. Phoned that agency and they gave me another number which led to an answering machine, no call back. So I continued to phone NSLSC to see if I could find out where my loan had been sent to.

"After phoning consistently for about two weeks, I finally was forwarded to somebody who claimed to be a supervisor at NSLSC. She seemed to understand, and she told me that my loan would be recalled to that office for a review and that everything would be worked out. Last I heard of that, and thus began the runaround 'your loan isn't at our office,' 'your loan hasn't been recalled,' 'your loan is in recall and you will receive a call on Monday,' 'it looks like your loan is still in recall,' 'we can't communicate with the people who do the recall,' 'sorry sir,' 'sorry sir,' 'sorry sir.' And finally, after another month of not being contacted, 'your loan has been sent to Vancouver sir.'

"WTF???? So now my loan is in Vancouver with an agency that claims to be HRDC. They can't really give me much information besides that I owe them money and they are willing to be nasty to get this money. My loan has somehow jumped from $19,000 to around $22,000 in the last year and a half of nonsense, interest I guess. Now if you read that and come out a little confused I hope you'll understand the confusion I'm under over this whole situation."

Replied kwelmm: "I hear ya! They always seem to be sorry, don't they! Sorry doesn't cut it. When are they going to learn that simple notion? 'Oh sorry, we have successfully f***ed you up for life....' and you can imagine them on the end of the line just smirking their little ol' faces off."

The ubiquitous Company T, mentioned in several of the previous posts, actually has a topic heading all its own on the site. Frustrated borrowers repeatedly accuse it of mishandling their accounts, forcing them incorrectly into delinquency or default, taking money when it wasn't owed, or other transgressions. A selection:

00Debbie00*: As most of you know when you place a call to the NSLSC (National Student Loan Service Center) 1-888-815-4514 the system asks you to put in your Sin#. At this point if you have a previous student loan in repayment or tax relief then the automated system promptly directs your call to [Company T]. However, if you simply press the # button twice you will be directed to the NSL Service Center.*

It is this redirecting to [Company T] that has caused me considerable grief. They are one of THE most incompetent agencies I have had the misfortune to deal with. I have had a repeat of the following events for more than a year now .....

- *the service center gives misleading or false information*
- *the service center omits important information*
- *the service center loses faxes and other paperwork repeatedly*
- *the service center does not record accurate information from telephone calls on their system*
- *the service center has reported inaccurate information on my credit history*
- *the service center has failed to send out vital documentation in a timely and efficient manner*

I can not express the stress and frustration that they have caused me. Since the Government has awarded them the contract I feel that this agency has become compliant in their dealings with student loan borrowers, failing to meet certain standards.

I would like this post to reflect the many individuals such as myself that have experienced such preventable and unnecessary complications with their student loans - so please, add your name to this list if you feel that [Company T] has reached a level of incompetence as I have described above. :)

tbeals: *Why oh why did I not read this a long time ago? I cannot put into words the frustration that I am experiencing applying for the RAP. Every time I call I put in my SIN and I get instantly forwarded. The people on the other end are all completely useless. Every time I call they tell me that my application will be processed in 2 business days. This process began July 2, 2010. Today is November 6, 2010. Still no resolution.*

I felt like the last person I talked to knew what she was talking about, and it seemed that something might actually happen, but still no approval or denial, and it's a week later. The time before last, the person on the phone refused to transfer me to a supervisor, because "they are only going to tell you the same thing I told you."

I will certainly be calling again on Monday, and I'll try the ## trick, and see if I get someone who knows what they're talking about.

FedUp: *WHY in your right mind would you input your SIN # to be forwarded? There needs to be a way that if you press * or "0" you are directed to a live person. I have spoken to numerous agencies including the CRA and NSLC and not once* have I given them my SIN#. They have confirmed it was me over the phone by other means such as my birthdate, where I live, some questions about where I worked and lived previously etc.... there is no need to give out your SIN# over an unsecured line.

Would you so willingly give out your credit card info?

00Debie00: *I appreciate your response Fed-Up but that is what the NSLSC system prompts the caller to do. If you call 1-888-815-4514 you will be prompted to select 1 for English and then asked to input your social insurance number followed by the # and then it will ask you for your pin number. You are then redirected pending your loan application status.*

PD: *It is illegal to use your SIN number for identification purposes. Do not input it or give it to them. SIN #'s are specifically to be used only for preparing Canada Revenue Agency slips (taxes). Phone the Executive Customer Service # 1-866-788-0388 for assistance. If you are dealing with RAP-PD (permanently disabled). Phone the regular #. Keep punching 0 until you get a live person. Do not give them any information no matter how many times and excuses they give you. Keep asking to be transferred to the Canada Student Loans program until they do.*

I am now delinquent on my account through no fault of my own. Have a history of mistakes being made on my file every six months. But never to the point of being sent to collections. I gave my SIN number but was transferred to [Company T] without my knowledge. After arguing with a moron for almost an hour, that was when she told me she was in that department. Her lack of knowledge of the program and outright lack of common sense was utterly amazing. The icing on cake was when she told me I was not disabled and had never applied for RAP-PD. Even though I am now on my third application under this program. She told me I had to prove my disability. They have no record of my being disabled. Gee, if I am not disabled why do they have to enlarge all communication and forms to 24 font. Why did I get grant money while going to school specifically for the permanently disabled? Duh.

Erika: *Hi, yeah, I was actually induced into being late for my payment when i did a DRAP application. They said that my payments would be put on hold until a decision had been made and then just kept stringing me along until the payment was a day late and sent it to [Company T]. I'm always curious to know who i'm dealing with so I did some research and it turns out that [Company T]is owned by [Company N], an American mega corporation that owns several student debt collection agencies, including the notorious Sallie Mae. [Company N] CEO's annual salary in 2009 was 5 million dollars. Obviously a company like [N] that's traded on the NYSE and is obviously profitable wouldn't bother buying [Company T] if it didn't think it could make money. I just wrote an article about this on my blog. I hope it's okay that I plugged. I'm really pissed off about this, seriously.*

00Debbie00: *I too had another upsetting discussion with a member of [Company T] this afternoon. Being disabled myself I asked the woman on the other end if she could speak up because I could not hear her. She then yelled very loudly "can you hear me now" in a condescending and sarcastic tone. I felt like jumping through the phone and strangling her but instead I yell back "yes" hahaha. Then to top it all off I asked her if the Provincial portion of my student loan had been processed and* she said no and that they had no record of my student loan. When I asked her if I could speak to someone else she simply said, "if you have lost it you will have to call another number to have it reissued". I was livid so I called my university only to learn that they had verified with Resolve that yes my application had been received and that funding would be sent to me promptly. I am still appalled at the severe level of incompetence of the regular staff at Resolve. My gawd, something has to be done about this.

crisist: Hi everyone, I am having the same issue here. I got a letter from [Company T] stating that I owe 94$ immediately. This was 2 months after I finished university. I already applied for repayment assistance before I received this letter. I called the NSLSC office and asked them what this letter was about. They said they have bad news....that the damage has been done to my credit score but that the repayment assistance program already covered the payment. they said this damage is repairable but it will take a longer time to repair this. in order for that to happen, I have to improve my credit score.

I wasn't able to make payments for my loans while I was in school, I was unemployed. I find this really unfair....and I feel from what everyone else wrote here, that nothing can be done about this.

00Debbie00: Hi Crisist,
I am sorry to hear you are having problems. I still have dealings with the NSLSC reporting inaccurate information on my credit history. I have written them repeatedly to correct the issue but it is no use. I get one person on the phone and she will tell me one thing then the next day I will get another person on the phone and they will tell me something totally different. I

have even requested they send the information in writing so that I have something to fall back on and STILL the people at NSLSC do not get it right. They don't know their ass hole from a fishing pole hahaha and I am the one that suffers for it. Once I find out the correct regulating office I will post the information here for you to use too.
Regards

crisist: Thanks for replying to my post. I can only imagine what you and everyone else is going through. I forgot to mention that Tricura also tried getting money out of my account and [Company T] is charging me 30$ for having insufficient funds in my bank account. It's illegal to withdraw money out of a person's account without my permission or notification. I am going to call these a***holes again today and yell at them for this. There's no getting through to them. They try to sound like smart ass es all the time, every agent you call, it's the same deal over again. And NSLSC is useless to talk to about this because they are misinformed bout [Company t]. In fact, a [Company T] agent told me that NSLSC "cannot speak on behalf of [Company T]" when I told [Company T] that NSLSC covered my missed payment through the Repayment Program. [Company T]said the payment wasn't covered and that I have to apply for their Repayment Program which is an Interest Relief Program. NSLSC told me that [Company T] handles the repayment program and that they are the department of NSLSC. Now I told this to [Company T] and they get all defensive and say NSLSC is separate from them and that I'm very confused and misinformed. Don't you think they should inform people of this information?

Well I wish you all the best in dealing with them and don't stop dealing with them. The other day I called them again and I hear their colleagues laughing and giggling in the background. I told my mom this and she said "they have fun while they make mistakes". So true. I hope [Company T] gets shut down.

00Debbie00: *When you sign your Student Loan document, whether electronically or in person, you are giving them the right to go into your account. You actually have to call them and tell them that you DO NOT give them permission to access your account for credit purposes. This will stop them from trying to take money out of your account. Hope this helps.*

Deb

Administrator: *And always a good idea to NOT use the account or bank where you deposited your student loans! Go to another bank!*
Administrator

00Debbie00: *I totally agree with the Administrator. When you set up your direct deposit use an account that you specifically set up for your student loan and nothing else. Have a separate account for your personal banking. :)*

There are a myriad ways in which being caught in the student debt gears can hurt borrowers, depending on individual circumstances. But the endless mixups, uncertainties, and, above all, the seeming lack of alternatives, of any way out of the maze, takes a toll on borrowers. Unlike homeowners, who can sell up and move to a rented room if the mortgage becomes too big a burden, or business owners who fall on hard times and must declare bankruptcy, students can't move away from their debt without leaving Canada altogether, or legally declare bankruptcy (at least for seven years). Even those who are paying back their loans run the risk, as so many of O'Meara's contributors have shown, of that not being enough to keep them out of trouble.

The result is a pervasive and constantly growing burden of emotional stress.

Detrimental impact

Noting that "debt and financial concerns are an extra psychological burden on top of the other pressures of university life," a 2004 British survey of thousands of students in the UK found that those with a high degree of financial worry felt more "tense, anxious or nervous," more "criticized by other people," and found it more "difficult getting to sleep or staying asleep" than students with low financial concerns. Even at low levels, the study concluded that debt "can have a detrimental impact on students' experience of university."[1]

The dry, matter-of-fact language of the study authors belies the emotionally bleak reality of contributors to O'Meara's site.

"I have huge student loan debt, which is slowly killing me," wrote Veristic. "I work three jobs, over 70 hours a week, and still can't keep up with loan repayments. I currently pay $1,500 in student loan repayments per month and I have fallen behind with rent and personal loans, resulting in ongoing calls for payment. Since I have a student line of credit and also old student loans, my payments are beyond my capacity. I called the banks that have taken over the old student loan debt, and they all said they cannot reduce the minimum monthly payments.

"I am working so hard, barely eating anymore, can't sleep, and think that there is no way to resolve this. I don't know how to fix this problem. Lately I have been thinking that suicide might be the only option because I can no longer cope with this debt."

"Hunter2" echoed this post, with marriage problems thrown in, and tried to offer advice:

From personal experience, I know the urge [to suicide] is there. Sometimes I think my family would be better off. We are facing a really serious debt situation and there is no possible way that I can make enough to pay down a $1,400 a month debt. I try to think about making little payments, doing small things, but it's unrealistic in some ways.

"My husband and I have had many arguments over my student loans. We were not together when I started school and were married after I completed. We have separated once over the issue and if collectors really start hammering me, well, I don't know how much he can handle. If I go into a depression again, that may well be the death knell for our marriage. When you are facing a mountain of debt with no job prospects that would come even close to enabling a payoff in your lifetime, it's easy to just want to escape. Especially combined with the feeling that everyone would be 'better off' without the stress of it.

"I had read a couple of years ago about a woman who owed the government $20,000 in back taxes (married with two young kids). She could not handle the stress and opted out. Her husband was heartbroken and started a media campaign against the government and collectors who he felt pushed her over the edge. It was really sad.......

"Things can change. I think the primary thing is holding on and not giving in to the urge. My hope lies in going to court and that's my focus. From reading documents, judges may not discharge the debt [in bankruptcy], but may reduce it, even [for] people who have been dishonest with the system, which I feel pretty good about because I have been truthful at all times. I feel I have acted in good faith and am documenting that aspect.

If they would reduce my debt to an amount that is plausible to pay back, I would happily (actually I would be thrilled) pay back say 20 per cent of my income per month for the next 10 years? Anyway, now I am rambling. Sorry........"

Reading these stories, even as the required research for a book, is depressing, but let's hear some more. It provides a sense of the sheer volume of misery out there–thousands of desperate young people. O'Meara said his site gets "anywhere from 1,000 to 3,000 hits a week." For each contributor, there are hundreds of "lurkers" with similar problems who read the posts, but don't themselves contribute.

"Nabma" wrote: "I felt compelled or obligated to go to school. Every single person in the school system said more schooling was the only possible route to get a job. I wanted to work for my first year, but was convinced by many people that school was the best choice. Personally, I'm single, no dependents and no co-sign to my debt...... I was 18 when I signed the loans, but was not an adult by a longshot. Now I am very poor, with all the other expenses which are necessities, so my tax returns and other random payments go towards my student loans. But in three years of paying over $10,000 to the government, my student loans went UP, yes UP. The interest added on because I wasn't paying regular amounts. So now my $20,000 student loans are now [still] $20,000. After paying 50 per cent off. That's all I need to hear to make a suicidal guy go off the deep end."

"Tillers" reported: "I'm very stressed with a student loan debt of $80,000. I left school due to medical problems, so never completed. Also ran out of funding. Canada Student Loans refused my interest relief application due to my inability to pay [an up-front lump sum] $2,000 of capitalized interest which they demanded in one week. I even offered payments, however, they refused. I recently went through bankruptcy just over a year ago. However, CSL was exempt. The monthly payment asked for by CSL is $700. My income is $2,000. Can they start withdrawing this from my account?"

"Noluckatall" added: "I requested the Repayment Assistance package last month. My loan has been arrears for nine months. So I called, and the guy said that it came to the proper address. Said next week, if they didn't get the papers they sent last month, I would be sent to collections.

"He said they will take away my income taxes and garnish my wages.

"I suffer from severe depression and anxiety........ I called a crisis line in February. She gave me the health unit. I guess I can call them tomorrow..... "I want to give up. I make barely enough to support myself. My income tax refund will only be $100. I'm not even done with school. I took time off because my mental health is so poor. My family can't help with money. I have huge credit card bills to pay off..... Just being in such dire straits and barely getting by, and then having this aloof, snide man from [Company T] tell me they will take my wages and income tax was the last straw. You know what I mean?

"If it weren't for the fact that my mother loves me, I would have killed myself long ago. If you want to flame me, go ahead. I give up."

Less than two weeks later, Noluckatall wrote again:

"Sigh. I logged onto my account and saw this message: 'We have received your application for Repayment assistance. However, your documentation is incomplete. We have sent you a letter advising what is required to complete your application form. Please respond as requested to prevent your application from being cancelled.'

"I sent in EVERYTHING. I used the checklist that they supplied. Watch it come too late and my application gets cancelled. This is absolutely bleeping ridiculous. I guess I will give them a call tomorrow......"

"BN" used fewer words to express the same frustration: "I don't know what to do. I am being harassed with collection agency's phone calls at work. Depressed and thinking about suicide. Vicious circle. Never ends. I will be getting out of the circle. I had enough."

Some of these posts are simply venting, and the writers likely wouldn't act on their impulses. But others may–and some have. In both Canada and the U.S., suicide is currently "the second leading cause of death among young people, after motor vehicle accidents,[2]" and debt is believed to be a factor in many cases.

In his 2007 U.S. best-seller, *Maxed Out*,[3] author James D. Scurlock tells the stories of two youngsters who cut their own lives short when debt became overwhelming. Both incidents were publicized in the U.S. media and were also featured in the film documentary version of Scurlock's book. Although neither student's debt was due directly to tuition payments, both had been targeted by credit sellers while on campus.

"Janne O'Donnell remembers when she took her son Sean to college. A National Merit Scholar from a small town in Oklahoma, Sean, she remembers, "was so excited to be in the big city, Dallas." He was only 18, she said, 'he didn't have a job. Who would give him a credit card?'"

That question, Scurlock writes, was "impossibly naive. Not only would they give him a credit card, they would practically shove it down his throat......

"Janne's son eventually dropped out of college. Sean moved back home and [found himself] working two minimum-wage jobs, paying down $12,000 in debt on 10 credit cards.....

He tried to figure out a way to declare bankruptcy, finish school, and somehow get a law degree, his dream. Living at home and working more low-wage jobs must have been humiliating for a National Merit Scholar who'd left for the big city with so much potential.... Sean told his mother he felt like a failure and two days later hung himself.......

"One day a collector called up and suggested that Janne should pay up to honor Sean's memory. 'I gave you my son,' she said. 'What more do you want?'"[4]

The second student, Mitzi [last name not given] "hanged herself in her dorm room after racking up a modest $2,500 in credit card debt (the young woman didn't leave a note, but did spread her credit card bills on her bed by way of explanation)."[5]

Alan Michael Collinge, in his book *The Student Loan Scam*,[6] described two other American students whose suicides were directly attributed to student loan debt:

"In September 2007, Jason Yoder, a 35-year-old recent graduate of Illinois State University, was found dead in a chemistry lab on campus–the same chemistry lab where he had done the research to complete his master's thesis. He had complained to relatives that he was feeling 'lower than low,' could not find a job, and that his student loans had grown to $100,000.

"As his mother was preparing for the funeral, she was harassed by collection calls from individuals wanting to know when he would pay up.

"Michele Guidoni also received his master's degree in chemistry. According to his mother, Gail, Michele was severely depressed because his student loans had grown to more than $200,000; he had consolidated them at a high interest rate and was unable to refinance the debt when the rates dropped. This hard-line rule became overwhelming for Michele, and on September 28, 2005, he shot and killed himself.[7]"

In Canada, Mark O'Meara describes several students and graduates who contributed to his CanadaStudentDebt website who were seriously suicidal. In each case, he first attempted to give them some online counseling, then phoned police and gave them the poster's computer IP addresses, from which a home address could be tracked, and advised them to pay the despondent contributors a call. One was saved by police intervention. But O'Meara never found out how the others fared. "The police don't always call you back in such cases."

The borrower posting in the most recent incident, in 2011, was older than many contributors to the list, but his predicament was representative:

"I was called 'grandiose' by the collector who called. People notice I'm not the same. They are cruel, calling names. I'm 53–it hurts like I was only seven. It convinces me I'll never keep a job or fit in. I wish I had never tried to make life better for myself through student loans. I would advise anyone who can't afford school to just don't go. These loans are signed in blood. You'll never be free–only one way. It's in the Act, the debt is extinguished upon death. So be it. I'm tired, older, depressed, in student debt, wife's on half income. The only time I leave the house is to feed my cigarette addiction. The rest of the time I sleep sleep sleep–very distraught, very depressed. Yesterday I tried the carbon monoxide solution: took a larger dose of my meds to try and pass out so I wouldn't leave the car in case I panicked. I guess there are too many holes in my garage and too much fresh air–I didn't do it right. I'm still here. Just now I yelled at my wife–I've never yelled at my wife– and swearing–I've never done that. The pressure on our marriage is the worst part of it all. The alleged debt is going to

ruin us. I don't know what else to do. Try again until I get it right I guess."

Also in Canada, credit counselor John Leblanc, whose firm, CFW Group Inc., specializes in helping people--particularly students--deal with credit problems, said: "I've had two Canada Student Loans clients in the past that have passed away, one to suicide and the other I don't know if it was intended or it was an accident. One guy in Ontario, he laid himself on the train tracks. Dead serious. It [student loan debt] was the stick that broke the camel's back. He had an outstanding student loan that I was helping him rectify, which was a long process."

He could not give the student's name because "the parents want to keep it quiet."

Desperate measures

Leblanc adds that suicide may not be the only act of desperation borrowers turn to.

"Another area of concern, and this is something I see, are students who are in the sex trade, trying to pay student loans. That's a very common issue in Toronto and B.C. In Canada, it's bad. There are a lot of young girls working in the escort industry and in Craig's List and all that, who are there because student loans are just draining them. Some of them are my clients."

Others support Leblanc's observations. For two years, Associate Professor Ada Sinacore of McGill University in Montreal, has been studying the phenomenon of students who pay for their education through sex work. "It's not something they are choosing because they think it's a great way to make a living," she said,[8] noting that such work can bring negative consequences during and after university. These include not developing their resume in their area of study, fear of being discovered and stigmatized by potential employers, and possible legal troubles or arrests. Not to mention the risk of contracting sexually transmitted disease, or being beaten or even murdered by a pimp or a customer.

Indeed, recent reports from England indicate an alarming number of student loan borrowers there are turning to "desperate and dangerous measures to pay for their education." According to Michael Holden, of Reuters news service:

"Desperate British students, faced with rising costs on the back of government austerity measures, are turning to prostitution, gambling and other dangerous pursuits to fund their studies, support workers and student leaders said on Wednesday.

"The English Collective of Prostitutes (ECP), a welfare body for sex workers, said it estimated the number of people approaching it for help had doubled in the last year as students struggled to make ends meet.

"'(The government) know the cuts and the austerity programs and the removing of grants, they know when they remove those resources it drives women further into poverty,' Sarah Walker from the ECP told Reuters.

"'The way that women survive poverty is often through sex work. The government knows that and they don't seem to care, frankly.'

"Young people have been the hardest hit by economic slowdown, with youth unemployment now accounting for 1.03 million of the 2.64 million unemployed, the highest level since 1992.

"Last year, the government said it would scrap the Educational Maintenance Allowance, a grant to older teenage schoolchildren to help them stay in education, and allow university tuition fees to treble up to U.S. $14,000 a year from 2012.

"With part-time jobs scarce and the cost of living being squeezed with rising prices, the National Union of Students (NUS) said young people were taking desperate and dangerous measures to pay for their education.

"'In some cases that's sex work, but we're also hearing about clinical trials, gambling.... dangerous work where there's very little, if any, kind of employment rights,' said Estelle Hart, the NUS's national women's officer.

"'You often hear it's very easy to get a bar job. Well it's not easy to get a bar job in this economic climate; it's not easy to get any job.'

"A study by researchers at a London university published last year found 16 per cent of students were willing to engage in sex work to pay for their education and 11 per cent would work for escort agencies.

"Ms. Hart said a recent study by Leeds University in northern England revealed 25 per cent of strippers and lap dancers were students. She said the government had a duty to investigate what effect its changes and cuts to education budgets were having. The prostitutes collective said women of all ages were affected and they were working in brothels, as strippers, in lap dancing clubs, and on sex phone lines.

"'It's right across the sex industry. With sex work, you can work for maybe one evening a week and make enough money to cover all your expenses,' Ms. Walker said. 'It's younger students who are just starting out in university and also women who are going back trying to get a degree or increase their skills.'

"She said the scrapping of the EMA allowance had badly hit some mothers.

"'When that money is cut, it's the mother who often has to make up for it,' she said. 'That is something that is driving women into sex work.[9]'"

Ron Roberts, one of the authors of the London University study cited by Hart, notes: "I think it used to be the case that people might have gone to university in order to avoid this kind of life. Now it seems like people are having this kind of life in order to go to university."[10]

The situation is not much different in Canada, says John Leblanc, adding: "Student loans are a devastation."

1. Cooke, Richard et al. "Student debt and its relation to student mental health." *Journal of Further and Higher Education*, Vol. 28, No. 1, February 2004.

2. Canadian Mental Health Association. "Reflections on Youth Suicide," as posted on the Canadian Children's Rights Council website, http://www.canadiancrc.com/Youth_Suicide_in_Canada.aspx

3. James D. Scurlock, *Maxed Out: hard times, easy credit and the era of predatory lenders* (New York: Scribner, 2007).

4. *Ibid.*, 63, 67.

5. *Ibid.,* 64.

6. Alan Michael Collinge, *The Student Loan Scam: the most oppressive debt in U.S. history–and how we can fight back* (Boston: Beacon Press, 2009).

7. *Ibid.*, 64.

8. Shadi Elien, "Debate sheds light on students in sex work," *Georgia Straight*, 29 April, 2010, as posted online at http://www.straight.com/print/320014.

9. Michael Holden. "Desperate British students 'turning to prostitution,' sex workers' group says," *Reuters* news service, as published in *The Globe & Mail*, online edition, 14 December 2011, http://www.theglobeandmail.com/report-on-business/international-new...

10. Shadi Elien, *Op.Cit.*

Chapter Four: Easy Meals

"What, wouldst thou have a serpent sting thee twice?"

–Shakespeare, *The Merchant of Venice*

In the wild, predators are quick to spot and target prey animals that are at a disadvantage, even a temporary disadvantage. Wolves and coyotes home in on deer weakened by hunger, or floundering in deep snow; foxes seek out wounded or sick rabbits that can't run as fast as their fellows. Hyenas will attack the newborn calves of wildebeests.

The hunters are also aware of the needs of the hunted, waiting in ambush, for example, near water holes where the herbivores must come to drink

In the socio-financial jungle that is modern North America, young people are automatically at a disadvantage--due to their inexperience--and their need for an education makes university campuses into so many water holes. They are natural prey.

But, to paraphrase Orwell, some seekers of knowledge are more vulnerable than others. In a field of easy meals, they are twice as easy, a walking temptation to double-dip.

Take Jasmin Simpson, for instance. The student loan system has made her pay more than twice as much as her fellows, because she is deaf, blind and has Systemic Lupus Erythematosis.

No Canadian equivalent

Lupus is a disease that causes the body's immune system to attack healthy cells and tissues, including the skin, joints, kidneys, heart, lungs, blood vessels and brain. It can be very painful, and often flares up without warning, making work or study impossible.

Simpson, now 36, was attending Gallaudet University in Washington, D.C., a liberal arts college designed specifically for deaf or hard-of-hearing students (Gallaudet, and the National Technical Institute for the Deaf, in Rochester, N.Y., are the only two universities in North America specializing in training deaf students. They have no equivalent in Canada).

Simpson was studying, first for a bachelor's degree in Social Work, and later for a master's, to prepare her to help other people like herself. Born in Korea and adopted by a family in Canada, where she grew up with other adopted Asian children with serious disabilities, she feels an obligation to give back in kind.

Then her Lupus flared up. She was forced to temporarily suspend her studies, in order to return to Canada for medical treatment. Following treatment, she had to reduce her course load.

At the time, her tuition and living expenses were being covered by a combination of federal and provincial student loans and Ontario Disability Support Program payments. She needed every penny. Gallaudet is an expensive school–it charges international students US$21,700 a year in tuition and US$9,860 for room and board.

"My family and I tried to explain to the [government] that I withdrew from Gallaudet because I needed medical treatment in Canada," says Simpson, speaking through an American Sign Language interpreter. "I had a very serious illness and tried to explain it. The National Student Loans Centre didn't care about my situation. They just pointed to 'policy.'"

Despite her attempts to show that her withdrawal from school was temporary, her student loan was cut off and "they penalized me with increased interest." She had to engage a lawyer, specialized in disability law, to battle the government to reinstate her loan.

Eventually, the provincial, but not the federal, part of her loan was reinstated, but that wasn't the end of the matter. Due to her forced absences and reduced course loads, Simpson needed five years to earn her bachelor's and three for her master's, a total of eight years to reach a point where a non-disabled student would be after six. And all of it at the high tuition rates of Gallaudet.

To be fair, the university's high costs were not due to gouging on its part. In 1989, the U.S. Congress imposed a surcharge on foreign students who attended Gallaudet and the National Technical Institute for the Deaf, and has so far resisted calls by advocates for the disabled to have the extra charge removed. Critics of the surcharge point out that there are no other such universities in North America, and thus many deaf students have two choices: attend Gallaudet or NTI, or forget about a university education. To levy such a surcharge, critics insist, is a violation of the United Nations Convention on the Rights of Persons with Disabilities.

Nevertheless, the surcharge remains.

In the past, disabled Ontario students' tuition (including the surcharge), books, supplies, transport to and from campus, the cost of Sign Language interpreters, skills assessment and training were covered by non-taxable grants from the Vocational Rehabilitation Services (VRS) program, co-funded by provincial and federal governments. Grants don't have to be paid back. In 1998, however, the Mike Harris Conservatives scrapped the program, with Ottawa's consent. Afterward, tuition for disabled students was provided in loan form, through the Ontario Student Assistance Program (OSAP) and Canada Student Loans, which did have to be paid back. And the loan was capped, at a maximum $10,000 per year, less than half Gallaudet's yearly tuition.

Prior to the 1998 changes, room and board expenses were covered by the government Family Benefits Allowance. After that year, they came under the Ontario Disability Support Program (ODSP), and a means test was imposed for qualification. Neither ODSP nor OSAP covered costs for interpreters, tutors, or any skills assessments. After 1998, any money going to the disabled also became taxable (the rule was later partly reversed). Finally, to continue to qualify for their support, students attending school outside of Canada were required to fill out and sign a battery of forms--not once, but four times a year. Simpson had to fax these, along with a photocopy of her passport, to the loans office. She also had to authorize her sister to deposit her provincial loan money in her bank account.

The extra years her illness forced Simpson to spend finishing school meant she was running up considerable additional expenses to earn her degrees--well over what a non-disabled student would have to pay. In fact, she estimates she's incurred roughly 60 per cent more student debt than a non-disabled student would have to obtain comparable credentials.

Of course, she is not alone. Thanks to the Congressionally-imposed tuition surcharge in the U.S., and the Harris government's scrapping of the VRS grants for tuition, hundreds of deaf students in Ontario and across Canada are in the same boat. Several provinces followed Ontario's example, cutting their support for the disabled (to their credit, Manitoba and Newfoundland remained honorable exceptions).

Enrolment figures for both Gallaudet and NIT make the result glaringly obvious: Between 1998 and 2009, Canadian student enrolment at NIT dropped by 82 per cent. At Gallaudet, between 1999 and 2010, it went down by nearly 60 per cent.

This rankled Simpson's sense of fairness. In 2007, she sued both the federal and Ontario provincial governments for the difference in cost, claiming that requiring disabled students to pay more for the same result violates the equality clause in the Canadian Charter of Rights. She hoped her case would set a precedent for others like her.

It must have been a public relations nightmare for the defendants, playing Goliath to Simpson's David in what looked to many observers like a clear case of bias. The government side quickly offered not only to make good on the extra 60 per cent Simpson was demanding, but to forgive her entire student loan debt. It also vowed to amend the alleged discriminatory provisions of the loans program.

Perhaps recalling the bureaucratic intransigence she encountered in her previous experience, when she'd first had to drop out of school temporarily, Simpson was wary of the government offer. While it would erase her own individual debt, the debts of other disabled students were not included in the deal, and government promises for the future were vague.

In 2006, the Harper government in Ottawa had abolished the $5.5 million funding of the federal Court Challenges Program, set up in the 1970s to provide financial help for key court cases that advanced language and equality rights. Simpson knew that, without such support, few if any disabled students would have the resources to bring a similar, future challenge.

Her suit might be the last chance to end what she saw as student loan discrimination.

Rather than immediately accept the tempting offer, she told her lawyer to seek a conditional agreement, stating that if the government's revisions to the loans program met her concerns over the rights of her fellow disabled students, she'd drop her suit. But if they didn't, she would pursue her Charter challenge.

"The government tried to settle out of court, offering me money," Simpson said. "I turned it down because I refuse to feel any guilt for friends also struggling with student loans. It is tempting to take the money to pay off my debt, but I chose to fight for people with disabilities. If I decided to take the settlement, no one [else] would take the case. I am concerned about the future of young students with disabilities."

A disappointment
The revisions turned out to be a big disappointment.

"In August 2010 [government] made some small improvements to their repayment program policies," Simpson explained. "However, some changes were hidden and made things worse. For example, the Permanent Disability Program became more strict than before."

The financial threshold for means testing was lowered, disqualifying students whose family incomes were deemed too high, even if the families were not contributing to the students' education. When deciding on loan repayment rates, government would look only at gross income, not net, ignoring disabled students' true financial situation after expenses. Students were also obliged to provide more information about medical expenses, with evidence in the form of copied receipts, along with copies of health insurance, rent and other bills. Student loan forms also had no space or box to explain why loans couldn't be repaid immediately, so students had to write a separate cover letter to explain, or else risk the sudden loss of their exemption.

In a classic "right hand gives, left hand takes away" strategy, government also agreed to reduce the amount of payments for borrowers with less ability to pay, but simultaneously raised the interest rate on these loans, reducing the amount of principal covered in each payment.

Simpson refused the government's proposal, and sent back the money government lawyers had offered. As the Toronto *Star's* Carol Goar reported:

"Federal lawyers, counting on a quick settlement, were surprised. They made a new offer. The government would erase Simpson's entire student debt, plus interest, and cover her legal fees (approximately $71,000). She still said no.

"They tried once more, offering a mediated settlement and hinting more funds were available. Again she refused.

"She and [her lawyer David] Baker proceeded on the assumption that the case was going to court.[1]*"*

At the time this book was being written, Simpson's case was still before the courts. Government lawyers had made several bids to derail it, first filing a motion trying to remove Simpson's lawyer Baker from the case, and then claiming that Simpson had somehow given up her right to sue when she agreed to review the government's changes to the law and decide whether they addressed her concerns about discrimination.

Such motions are standard practice in any lawsuit, and a reason why many plaintiffs abandon their efforts. Each motion and counter motion takes up the court's time and lawyers' hourly-billed attention, driving up court costs and legal bills for both plaintiffs and defendants. It's a bit like upping the ante in poker. Even long-shot motions that have little hope of success make it harder for anyone with limited resources to "stay in the game." Some lawyers also use them as part of a scatter-gun strategy, hoping that if they throw enough motions at the opposition, one may eventually stick.

At some point, either side may conclude they're involved in a mug's game, and agree to settle.

Simpson, however, showed no sign of being ready to throw in her hand. It wasn't just about her, and she had allies and considerable evidence to support her efforts. Both the Canadian Hearing Society (CHS) and the Council of Canadians with Disabilities (CCD) were firmly behind her.

"Ms. Simpson's case clearly demonstrates there are built-in headwinds for persons with disabilities in the Canada Student Loan Program," said CCD Coordinator Laurie Beachell, "If persons with disabilities are to enjoy equal opportunity in post-secondary education, this discrimination needs to end."

"Unless you are disabled, you can have no idea how challenging it is for us to secure the education necessary to achieve independence and dignity in this country," said Hearing Society President Chris Kenopic. "If the pre-1998 program had not been in place, I wouldn't be sitting in this [president's] chair, because I could not have attended university. CHS calls on the federal government to stop litigating against Ms. Simpson and address the discrimination in the CSLP."

North America's first deaf Parliamentarian, Gary Malkowski, who served as a New Democratic Party (NDP) Member of the Ontario Provincial Parliament during the Bob Rae administration, also supported Jasmin's fight. A graduate of Gallaudet University in its pre-Congressional surcharge days, he sees the current student loans system in Canada as discriminatory and insists on "the removal of barriers to higher education." In a commencement speech at Gallaudet in 2011, he noted that "today, we have many deaf and hard of hearing professionals–doctors, lawyers, leaders–Dr. Alan Hurwitz, Gallaudet University, Gerry Buckley, National Technical Institute for the Deaf, Benjamin Soukup, Communication Services for the Deaf, and Chris Kenopic, the Canadian Hearing Society–all presidents and CEOs," and added that none of their careers would have been possible without access to university.

Both the Hearing Society's research and that of independent investigators bolster Simpson's case that current educational policy discriminates against the disabled.

A CHS statistical survey in 2004[2] concluded that "deaf.... students are unable to commence or continue their post-secondary studies in Canada or the United States"[3] for a variety of reasons. Among them were:

"Rising tuition costs.

"Dramatic changes or reductions in government funding:
– changing from grants to loans;
– imposing taxes on disability-related supports and out-of-country bursaries for students with disabilities."[4]

The report noted that Ontario had recently terminated funding for "computerized note taking and Sign Language interpretation services for deaf students attending public post-secondary institutions," while funds for similar services in private vocational schools had been continued, these were "limited to a maximum of one credit course per semester."[5]

An independent review was conducted for the Higher Education Quality Council of Ontario in 2011,[6] and one of its authors, Tony Chambers of the Ontario Institute for Studies in Education (OISE) at the University of Toronto, prepared a submission for the court as evidence in Simpson's case. At the time this book was written, the court had not yet considered his submission, which called particular attention to the findings that:

. "A student with a disability with a reduced course load of 40 per cent could take 10 years to complete a standard four-year university undergraduate degree–six years longer than his/her peers taking a 100 per cent course load. These additional years lead to extra expenses due to tuition increases, inflation, and living and transportation costs. These costs are compounded by the reality that very few national scholarship, award, and bursary programs take into account the reduced course load held by students with disabilities.....[7]

. "An astonishing 60 per cent of students with disabilities surveyed on-line believed that financial costs would influence the completion of their studies[8]........ In addition 26 per cent of students said they would like to continue their education beyond their current program but have decided to discontinue further educational pursuits due to debt level accrued through their present degree.....[9]

. "Couple their extended enrolment time trajectory with limited and restricted postgraduate labor opportunities, and their concern about incurring and repaying significant educational debt is further exacerbated."[10]

Invisible disabilities

Not all student disabilities are as physically obvious as being deaf or blind. Some young people face obstacles that are invisible, but just as hard–in some cases harder--to handle. They are made even worse by the complexity of the loans system, and the attitudes of the lenders, bureaucrats and debt collectors with whom student borrowers and their families must deal.

Rena del Piede Gobbi is a film maker, who earned her Bachelor of Fine Art, and more recently her Master of Applied Art, degrees in British Columbia. Her work is highly experimental and cutting-edge, as well as socially engaged. She has two disabilities, one physical, the other mental: a double whammy.

"I got bilateral tendonitis and lost the use of my hands during the [undergraduate] program," Gobbi said. "It's a permanent thing, in that I can't work full time on computers. I have to monitor how long I'm on a computer every day and really make sure I rest my hands. My doctor wrote it up as a secondary permanent disability."

In addition, she explained, "I have bipolar disorder, and it's severe. I have a depressive side, a manic side and hallucinations.

"My master's thesis was about the missing and murdered women from the downtown east side of Vancouver. I made a film. I went out and photographed the last places that a number of women were seen, and also things that play a key part in their disappearances, like a rendering factory, and one of the stores where [convicted multiple murderer Robert] Pickton sold his pigs. I didn't go out to the pig farm. I was just staying in that [east side] area.

"What I tried to do is look at ideas of authorship, and say I'm not a woman who lives on the street, but because these things happened in my life[time] and I'm living in the same area, I relate to their plight. And these are the things that cause me to feel a relationship to them, to want to make this film.

"Parts of it are autobiographical. Also, I'm trying to re-contextualize the city of Vancouver as culpable for the murders. In the film, there are images of the police station and City Hall, kind of backwards and standing still, when everything else is moving really frenetically. I'm trying to convey things through the speed of the film and through the images themselves, rather than through a story line. There's no dialogue in the film. It's 35 mm. It's beautiful.

"My work is all about doing things from an intuitive point of view. The idea is that when you watch this film, there is actually an effective synesthesia happening. Audience members are taken into a place within their own bodies and are feeling things and experiencing things within themselves."

Gobbi's success in achieving this effect is vouched for by the fact that her previous experimental films have been featured in no fewer than 15 film festivals worldwide.

Her thesis is titled *The Transmutation of Visceral Desecration: marginalized women, murder and the environment, contextualized in film.*

Which, of course, means absolutely squat to Canada Student Loans.

"When I graduated with my bachelor's, I had a student loan debt of about $26,000," Gobbi said. "I managed to get that first $26,000 forgiven through the student loan disability forgiveness program [at the time, this was possible for disabled students who could demonstrate certain conditions of financial hardship]. That took a really long time, because during the process I knew that I wanted to do a master's degree. I was applying to different schools to get into a master's program.

"I knew that I could get my [bachelor's] student loan written off, but I was afraid because they wouldn't tell me if I would still be able to get a student loan for the master's. They basically wouldn't say if I would ever be able to get approved for another loan."

There were no available grants sufficient to cover further schooling, and she had no financial resources other than student loans– which was why her original debt could be forgiven. But would getting that first debt written off preclude future help?

"That actually is the policy now," she continued. "If you get one loan written off for disability purposes you will not be able to take out another [federal] student loan. That's been the policy for about four years."

At the time of Gobbi's graduation this strict policy hadn't yet been adopted. Bureaucrats may have suspected it was coming, however: "I asked them over and over and over again, if I get this loan forgiven will I be able to take out another loan to do my master's? They wouldn't give that information. They would say, 'We can't give you an answer. We don't know the answer to that question.' I used to transcribe my conversations with them. I was having so much trouble with them that I would actually write down the name [if any was given] of the person I was talking to, the date, all of that information, every time I spoke to Canada Student Loans. It was quite strenuous dealing with them."

Part of the stress was due to the Catch 22 aspects of the program, and part to the size of the debt itself.

Gobbi's situation was complicated. If a disabled student was temporarily unable to find work or afford payments after graduation, they might qualify for interest relief, as well as a delay in their payment due date. Every six months, the borrower had to file papers showing his or her income and employment status, and so long as these kept coming and demonstrated hardship, the government would pay the interest on the loan for those six months and delay payment of the principal.

Part of a disabled borrower's income might come from social services disability support payments. A social services recipient could also work, but if he or she earned more than $500 per month in wages, support payments were docked. And,

Gobbi explained, "if you do get a job and make that $500 a month, then all of a sudden you have to start paying back the student loans. Your debt load is so high that it makes it really frightening to try to get a job. One person I was talking to was a single mother. She'd put her rent money in the bank and student loans would just take it out. It was brutal."

However, if a borrower could demonstrate permanent disability and meet certain conditions, the loan principal itself might eventually be forgiven. This is what Gobbi wanted to do, but not if it meant being unable to continue towards a master's degree.

As it turned out, at the time she was hoping to go on for her master's the policy permitted a second student loan, even if the previous one had been written off. But she didn't know that, and no one would tell her.

"They wouldn't tell me if I could get another loan," she said. "So I just kept on filing the paperwork every six months. You have to get a letter from Canada Pension Plan, and a letter from social services and fill out forms. I had a mental health advocate help me with that. But it went to the point where I ran out of the time that you're allowed to spend on [temporary] interest relief. I had to make a choice. I didn't have money to make the loan payments. I was in a state, totally stressed out."

Those who are unfamiliar with mental illness might simply shrug and think, "so what? So she's stressed." But for people with bipolar disorder the consequences of stress are of an entirely different level of magnitude, compared to what they would be for those without her condition. Sufficient stress, coming at the peak of a depressive cycle in the disease, could easily trigger suicide. Where this disorder is in play, stress is not a slow, silent killer, but a sudden, overwhelming one. It is–immediately and directly–life threatening.

"I went in to the mental health advocate [for help] and I did it, got the original loan forgiven. I was devastated. I thought that I was no longer going to be able to do my master's, that time had run out. And I'd applied five times to do my master's. It was a stressful thing to go through, with this thing hanging over your head. I didn't know if I could go on for a master's, until I re-applied to school, and then my [new] student loan was approved."

She had just squeaked in under the wire, however, before the policy was changed. As the rules stand now, a disabled student starting at bachelor's degree level cannot request loan forgiveness after graduation, if he or she intends to continue on towards a higher degree. The student must remain in school, and continue higher level courses in unbroken sequence, through to whatever terminal degree is envisioned.

This means that there are no second chances for the disabled. If a borrower gets a bachelor's degree and then has the loan for that bachelor's forgiven, they are prohibited from returning to school for a master's or doctorate. At the age of 21 or 22, when they graduate, they must act as if they know in advance that they will never wish to acquire further education–unless, of course, they are able to pay for it themselves.

This would have prevented the author of this book, had I been disabled, from returning to school for a graduate degree in my 50s, and subsequently starting a new career as a university professor. I received my bachelor's when I was 24.

"The system discourages people," said Gobbi adding that sometimes it feels as if "it's built specifically to stop people from getting off disability."

Mother's view

Disabled student borrowers aren't the only ones who feel the effects of the system. Their families are also hurt, especially single mothers like Susan [not her real name] who, herself a sufferer from bipolar disorder, must look on while her similarly-challenged son does battle with the bureaucrats. The son, call him Stan, is an unusually talented artist, whose oil paintings are not only highly original, but carry a sometimes disturbing emotional wallop. Though not yet finished with his fine art degree at a prestigious university, he already shows a mastery of composition and color normally seen only in older, far more experienced artists. Intelligent as well as talented, he had worked part-time in retail prior to his illness and done so well that he was promoted to a managerial position.

His disorder, formerly known as "manic-depression," seems to be associated with high-performing people, often those with genius or near-genius level intelligence. The list of known or suspected sufferers from the illness includes novelists Ernest Hemingway and Graham Greene, actresses Margot Kidder and Carrie Fisher, conductor Otto Klemperer and, more recently, both Margaret Trudeau and Amy Winehouse. Historians have speculated that Abraham Lincoln may have been so afflicted. The disorder can be controlled successfully with medication, but it is sometimes difficult to establish the correct dosage.

"He was in school up until 2008," Susan recalls. "And then he started to fall apart. He just started to unravel."

She knew the signs only too well, from her own and her parents' experience with the disorder, which is most probably genetic in origin. A writer and critic of the medical system, she has an above-average understanding not only of this particular malady and its treatment, but also of the medical bureaucracy and society's attitudes toward mental illness.

Stan had completed the fall 2007/winter 2008 school year, during which his family covered tuition costs, and was scheduled to take a couple of additional courses over the summer, for which he had applied for a student loan. He got the loan, but never got a chance to take the courses.

"He called me, and he was sick," his mother recalled. "There were many horrible things that were happening. He thought people could hear his thoughts. He phoned and said: 'I don't know what to do. I can't go out in the street; people are hearing my thoughts. I can't go on the subway. What can I possibly do?'

"He went into a psychosis," she explained, adding that while such symptoms are usually associated with schizophrenia, "you can be bipolar and get that. He was anorexic. He was 65 pounds lighter, but was doing hundreds of pushups a day, and walking everywhere [to lose more weight]. He started smoking, and he'd never smoked before. He shaved his hair bald. He got really, really sick. He was severely sick. He was institutionalized that summer."

At one point, she added, "he had seizures because the medications were wrong that they were giving him. It was a reaction to the medication."

Because he was in hospital, Stan couldn't attend classes, and despite his mother's attempts to explain to the university why he couldn't attend classes or come in to school and sign forms to formally withdraw, when the deadline for dropping courses passed, he was stuck with paying the full tuition. He did so with student loan funds. "They [the university] didn't care," said Susan. "They said 'he's missed the deadline, sorry.' We were on the hook for about $800."

This, in the world of student loans, was a relatively small amount, but Stan's situation subsequently became more complicated, and it wasn't long before the loan factor–small amount notwithstanding--became problematic as well.

If a student ceases his or her studies, within six months any outstanding student loans become due. However, as noted in Rena del Piede Gobbi's case, if the withdrawal is temporary and for medical reasons, regulations permit a student to apply for interest relief, while the loan is held in abeyance. The student must re-qualify for this relief at continuing six-month intervals by filling out forms and providing proof of his or her medical condition.

Simple, unless you're illness is psychiatric and you are embroiled in serious difficulty getting treatment, as well as trying to qualify for disability support–and unless you run up against a situation that scores of contributors to O'Meara's CanadaStudent Debt website refer to as the "Student Loan Service Centre (SLSC) Runaround."

Stan was faced with all of the above.

"He was in terrible rough shape, had lost contact with his original psychiatrist, and really hated the people at the place where he was hospitalized because he felt they were just trying to drug him [with the drugs that had caused his seizures]," recalled Susan. By that time, she had moved to another city in the same province. "So he came here, and the hospital was supposed to give him a referral." But the referral, which would have allowed him to get treatment in the new city, didn't come. Neither did the separation papers from his former part-time employer, which were needed for him to apply for disability support.

"After three months, finally, his employer sent the separation papers, so we could get minimal disability money for him. The hospital where he'd been treated kept saying 'we'll refer you, we'll refer you.' That started in September, and in late January or early February we finally got this referral to a hospital in [the new city]. I went there and filled out forms, and he filled out forms, and then they said 'you don't qualify for our program; you have to go back to scratch.'

"I've been through the mental health system, so it didn't surprise me. But it was really demoralizing for him. I was always keeping him from, you know, suicide isn't the answer. But after that day it was horrible. We went through all this and it was terrible, and then eventually we connected with his original psychiatrist, that he'd had since he was 12, who was very good. I said, 'I don't care how much the train fare costs, I'll pay the fare'" back to their original city.

"At that point it was coming up to six months, when they [student loans] want your money. I'm not stupid. I investigated and realized that he was allowed an exemption. Using that, we went to the loan system and they said 'OK, you get another six months,' but it would be reviewed. So these second six months were fine. They said they weren't adding interest.

"Then we started getting these papers to fill out." She held up a sheaf of letters and forms. "We filled them out. Here's a blank one. They were like this, for family income and so forth. We'd fill them out, this whole bunch, look at that! And send them in. Then they'd send you something back that said 'we cannot process your application [to renew the interest relief exemption].' But they wouldn't tell you what was wrong. They wouldn't tell you why they couldn't process the application. A box would be ticked and it would say 'please contact such and such an office immediately.' You can see at the top, here's the number to call. And you call, and you get put on hold. And I'd wait on hold and hold and hold, maybe 45 minutes. Then someone would answer and say 'we'll call you back.' But they wouldn't call back, so you'd have to phone again.

"Then they'd tell you you've filled the forms out wrong, but they wouldn't specify what was wrong."

She showed a set of forms, which could be filled out four possible ways. Since no one at the Student Loan Service Centre would say which of the four ways was correct, she explained: "We did it four times, four different ways. I faxed them four copies, with a cover letter explaining that, since they wouldn't tell us which was correct, they could take their pick. They had the fax. Then they said they needed another fax. And we sent them another. This was over three months.

"And then they just said, 'no, you don't have the right form to begin with.'

"Didn't have the right form! But it was the form they'd sent us earlier and told us to fill out! I'd say, 'OK, we need the right form. Send us the right form. Please fax us the right form.' And we never got--no matter how many times we asked--the right form! This was madness. I mean, normally I don't send faxes with four copies of the same form, ticked off four different ways, and a cover letter. They just said, you have to start again, and it's three or six months or whatever again, so 'we have to add more interest.' They'd say you had to call some other number, or some other person.

"Or they'd say: 'Yes, that's good. There's another cycle coming. We have your information. We'll be getting back to you.' And no one would get back to us. No one. Nothing would be mailed. Nothing came back saying anything that made sense."

At first, the National Student Loan Service Centre was dealing directly with Stan, with his mother in the background, helping him sort things out. But his illness worsened, and at the same time so did the behavior of the NSLSC telephone staff.

"The interest harassment didn't start till later," Susan said. "But then they started calling and calling. And Stan was so depressed. They'd ask to talk to him, and he'd pick up the phone and he'd say to me 'I'm getting this screaming person.' It was totally bizarre. They kept calling and calling, and his doctor was telling him he was near suicidal. He was so sick of them he'd just hang up the phone, shake his head, and come upstairs and lie down on his bed and cry. And he'd call them back and get another horrible, screaming person. And he'd come away and be depressed. He'd be gone for two or three days. He'd given up, and I felt I had to shield him from it. I asked his psychiatrist what we should do. He said 'keep him away from all stressors.'

"Finally I said he can't talk to these people. That was when I requested permission to talk for him. I asked for it but didn't get permission the first time within the deadline [to qualify for continued interest relief]. But I got it the second time. We had to send more faxes for that. And then I started getting these screaming people. I'd reply: 'Excuse me, you can't talk to me this way. If you talk to me this way I need to know your name and your number.' And they'd hang up. This after I'd been on hold for 45 minutes waiting to talk to them. You'd have some shrieking character, demeaning you. They were horrible. They'd use swear words. I'd say, 'what is your name? Spell it. Who is your manager.' And they'd hang up. This was the Student Loan Service Centre. They identified themselves as the National Student Loan Service Centre, or just NSLSC.

"I thought, OK, this must be insanity. The last two times they called and screamed, I just let them have it, and they hung up. It still didn't stop these calls. We just stopped picking them up. We had a year of this. It was horrible. I felt so aggressive and upset."

As a disabled person, who had withdrawn from school temporarily due to ill health, Stan should have qualified for interest relief, and had actually done so the first time around. Since then, he and his mother had tried hard to provide the proper documentation to continue qualifying. To no avail. Stymied by the "NSLSC Runaround," their deadline had passed.

Where formerly they couldn't get anyone to send a written explanation of what was wrong with their forms, or get an explanatory call back, now the calls and letters began streaming in–demanding payment.

"They came every other day, it seemed," Susan recalled. "They were relentless. On the telephone they claimed we had defaulted. They said it on the phone to me. But they never sent any official notice.

"I finally caved," she said. "I paid off his student loan just to shut them up. And I thought this number, $150 something, should be our interest, but no. They wouldn't let us off the hook. They said the total was something like $300."

In the end, after more than a year, the NSLSC would have continued hounding Stan and his mother, and risk driving him to suicide, over a difference of $150.

"He was designated someone who was not well because of depression, and they knew it!" Susan exclaimed, eyes blazing. "I wouldn't let that [suicide] happen, of course," she added. "But if he hadn't had me? I guess he's lucky to have me."

Even after the debt was paid, she added, shaking her head, "they still came after us, and called and called–for surveys! They kept calling for surveys, saying 'Where is he?' I kept saying 'He doesn't want to talk to you.' And then I'd worry: if he wants another loan in future, if he's not answering these surveys, is it going to affect him?'"

Eventually, Stan's health improved and he was able to return to school. And, because the family had repaid the original loan, plus interest, he could qualify for a new student loan. Penalizing Stan over the first loan was "outrageous," Susan said. "But he's better. He wants to go back to school. And they [the university] won't let you back unless your student loans are paid. That's one reason why I paid. I don't know what's going to happen to him in the future without an education. He can't cope without that."

She paused, and her voice broke.

"And now he's got another student loan. He's now considered an independent person, and my income is so low I don't factor into it. So he's $14,000 in the hole to these people. And it's scarey." Tears were falling from her eyes. "And he has another year to go............"

British teacher Peter Halstead, who teaches students with learning disabilities, recently contributed an article to the Manchester *Guardian* newspaper, and what he said applies as well in Canada as in the UK:

"I don't see it as a political matter of left versus right, but as a matter of conscience. If we believe that the measure of a society is found in how we treat our weakest and most helpless citizens, then I am saddened and embarrassed to be a part of this one."[11]

1. Carol Goar, "Goar: the high price of a trailblazer," *The Toronto Star*, 9 June 2011, as posted online at www.thestar.com/opinion/editorialopinion/article/1006019–goar...

2. The Canadian Hearing Society, "Status Report on Deaf, Deafened and Hard of Hearing Ontario Students in Post-Secondary Institutions: statistics, current trends, barriers, recommendations," February 2004.

3. *Ibid.*, 1.

4. *Ibid.*, 2.

5. *Ibid.*, 3.

6. Chambers, T., Sukai, M. And Bolton, M., "Assessment of Debt Load and Financial Barriers Affecting Students with Disabilities in Canadian Post-Secondary Education–Ontario Report," (Toronto: Higher Education Quality Council of Ontario, 2011).

7. *Ibid.*, 42-43.

8. *Ibid.*, 56.

9. *Ibid.*, 66.

10. *Ibid.*, 69-70.

11. Peter Halstead, "It saddens me to see young, vulnerable people having their lives made harder," *The Guardian*, 21 January 2012, as posted online at

www.guardian.co.uk/commentisfree/2012/jan/21/young-vulnerab...

Chapter Five: Collateral Damage

*"You take my house when you do take the prop
that doth sustain my house."*

–Shakespeare, *The Merchant of Venice*

Individual students, graduates and their families aren't the only ones hurt by an educational system increasingly based on profit, rather than on the pursuit of knowledge and the public good. When federal transfer payments for education are cut back, provincial education budgets trimmed, and tuition fees hiked, the burden of financing post-secondary education falls not only on our indebted youth but on society at large.

In curtailing a generation's future, the system simultaneously curtails the social options of all of us. The consequences may be consciously intended, or unintended and unforeseen, but in the long term they are unavoidable.

Take law, for example. In a democratic country, based on the Rule of Law, every citizen ought to have equal access to the courts and to legal representation. A level legal playing field is supposed to be part of the "fairness" picture.

But the reality is anything but fair, as Supreme Court of Canada Chief Justice Beverly McLachlin warned, in a 2007 call-to-action speech to the Canadian Bar Association.

A basic right

Declaring access to justice "a basic right," she said the justice system has become too expensive and complex for most

Canadians, adding that there is "no point" in having a system that nobody can afford to use. A Toronto *Star* journalist reported her speech:

"*The justice system risks losing the confidence of the public when 'wealthy corporations,' or the poor who qualify for legal aid, have the means to use the court system, [McLachlin] said, noting that for 'middle class' Canadians, resolving a legal problem of any significance often requires taking out a second mortgage or draining their life savings.....*

"*A Toronto Star investigation this year determined the cost of a routine three-day civil trial in Ontario to be about $60,000, more than the median Canadian family income....*

"*While high hourly rates charged by lawyers are part of the difficulty–up to $800 an hour in Toronto–the access to justice problem is complicated.*"[1]

McLachlin's warning assumed that it was middle class Canadians who were suffering, while "the poor" had access to justice through Legal Aid. In fact, both Legal Aid and so-called *pro-bono publico* (donated without charge, "for the public good") legal work are in jeopardy in Canada, and have been for some time.

Legal Aid depends in most provinces on government support, and that support has been plummeting provincially, as well as nationally through cuts in Canada Social Transfer payments. Writing in *Canadian Lawyer Magazine* in October 2010, Robert Todd reported that: "Legal Aid funding in Ontario–the province that spends the most on it per capita–fell by nearly 10 per cent from 1996 to 2006........ The result is palpable: according to Legal Aid Ontario's 2006-7 business plan, the number of people refused service had increased by 42 per cent in two years."[2]

He quoted New Democratic Party (NDP) Justice Critic Joe Comartin as calling "cuts to Legal Aid in British Columbia, for example, 'quite horrendous.' According to one estimate, funding in the province plummeted to $74 million in 2008-9, from $96 million in 2001-2. The B.C. Legal Services Society was forced to shutter five regional offices last year and lay off more than 50 staff due to the shortfall."

As a result of such cuts, Legal aid work is notoriously low-paid, with Ontario lawyers making between $97 and $106.90 per hour.

In an earlier, 2006 report on Legal Aid decline for the Canadian Bar Association, Legal Aid Ontario President and CEO Angela Longo was quoted as saying "a key challenge is the declining participation of the private Bar, with the number of private lawyers accepting Legal Aid cases down by nearly 30 per cent over the past five years. This is despite two modest increases to the hourly rates paid to lawyers, but they followed sharp reductions in funding that began in the mid-1990s–the impact of the 1996 reductions are still being felt."[3]

In his *Canadian Lawyer* article, Robert Todd quoted Ontario lawyer Jordan Weisz on the sort of sacrifices young, idealistic lawyers must make to take on Legal Aid work:

"All told, Weisz says he's still enthusiastic about criminal defence work. But the 'sad truth' is that he wouldn't do it if he were entering the profession at this moment. 'I don't think I could support myself,' he says..... Many [young lawyers] are forced to live and work out of bachelor apartments, renting an office a couple of days a week to meet with clients. They forego expenses that many view as mandatory–such as a secretary and library–in hopes of making ends meet doing the work they too love, without the mentorship and resources many believe they need to do it well."[4]

So difficult is it to find lawyers willing to take Legal Aid cases, that Ontario officials had to make more than 200 calls before they could find a lawyer to defend a man charged in a 2009 murder case. They finally found a lawyer–who had never participated in a murder trial.[5]

As for pro bono service, it's even harder to find lawyers willing to work for nothing. Saskatchewan Children's Advocate Bob Pringle reported that in 2010 the Children's Advocate Office asked for a pro bono lawyer to help children 62 times. In 38 cases the request was turned down because no lawyers were available. The Advocate's Office is an independent agency that looks out for children who are in government care.[6]

Children, in fact, are one of the groups who suffer most when Legal Aid staff, or pro bono volunteers, aren't available to represent clients. Another group are people involved in family law cases, especially women like the mother described by journalist Tracey Tyler:

"Terrified of losing custody of her children and in need of a good lawyer, Anne Singleton was stuck with an advocate who had never been to law school and had an irregular heartbeat induced by stress. That advocate was Singleton herself, a 46-year-old, part-time high school teacher facing an aggressive lawyer representing her estranged husband.

"'I was feeling very powerless,' said Singleton, who was in no condition for courtroom combat after the collapse of what she describes as an abusive marriage. 'I was feeling ashamed and full of self-doubt. I was a mess.'

"Six years of legal battle eventually wore Singleton down to the point of surrender and she agreed to set aside a restraining order against her husband and grant him joint custody of their two children.

"Her story is not uncommon. Singleton, who asked that her real name not be used, is one of an expanding legion of

Canadians who try to navigate the justice system without lawyers.[7]

In Ontario, Tyler noted, "one out of every three people who apply for Legal Aid in family law cases gets turned down."[8]

A no-brainer
And what has all of this to do with student loan debt? It's elementary:
Depending on which university they attend, and what their non-tuition living costs may be, law students in Canada who aren't rich enough to pay cash for their education can expect to graduate with a loan debt in the neighborhood of $150,000 to $250,000. Upon graduation, that brand-new lawyer will start looking for work to pay off the debt. If you owed that much, and were faced with the choice of applying for a job at a firm whose senior staff make $800 an hour, or for a job with Legal Aid that starts at $97 an hour, with a maximum of $106.90 (Jordan Weisz, mentioned above, makes that much, but when he factors in operational costs, nets only about $36 per hour[9])-- which would you pick?

Right. As they say in the States, a no-brainer.

A 2003 report by the Canadian Bar Association put it in writing. While acknowledging that "poor funding of Legal Aid" is part of the problem, it added that: "It seems obvious that debt burdens make it impossible for students to choose Legal aid as their path of choice."[10]

Tuition and student loan debt aren't solely to blame for the Legal Aid/pro bono lawyer shortage, but they sure don't help.

They're also a factor in student choices regarding other law specialties, as well as their choice of geographical location for future practice. In 2003, University of Toronto Provost Shirley Neuman submitted a study to the university on accessibility and career choice in the Faculty of Law,[11] to which the just-mentioned Canadian Bar Association report was a response. The CBA took issue with some of the Provost's assumptions and conclusions, but agreed with some of her data.[12] Though these two reports are a bit outdated, they clearly describe what are still problem areas today, and will be in future, as the projections of the Office of the Chief Actuary cited in Chapter One indicate.

"Data on career choice begins on page 23 of the Provost's study," wrote the Bar Association authors, "where it is noted that most U. Of T. Students choose to article in large firms and most graduates choose to start their careers in large firms. Over the study period, this trend has increased, with far less numbers going to small firms." The number of students opting for large firms rose from 20 per cent in 1995 to 38.7 per cent in 2000. As large firms tend to be "located in the large urban centres," this meant a corresponding shift away from choosing to practice in small towns or rural areas, threatening the latter with being under-served.

Also affected was the number of students interested in taking jobs in the area of public

interest law, or positions with non-profit organizations, as opposed to working in, say, the very profitable area of corporate law. Noting that the high costs of legal education could be "encouraging individuals to choose career paths that may not be their primary interest but have been selected for predominantly financial reasons,"[13] the CBA cited a literature review attached to the Provost's report, which pointed out: "Women are more likely to enter law school with not-for-profit career plans, but law school disproportionately shifts their preferences toward for-profit jobs."[14]

The CBA's authors saw initial entrance barriers to law school as a problem equal to, if
not greater than graduates' eventual career choices:

"The CBA Standing Committee on Equality is persuaded that significant increases in tuition fees [and consequent student debt], unless they are substantially mitigated by other programs which will encourage entrants to come forward, will harm us all in our efforts to ensure that the student body of law firms, and therefore of the Canadian legal community in the future, is reflective of the society which it serves......... [15]

"The least that can be said is that increasing tuition fees at this time will contribute in no way to increasing the racial and cultural diversity of the legal profession or the numbers of those interested in seeking careers in smaller or less urban law firms or in public interest law." [16]

The paper went on to add:

"It is common knowledge that the legal profession is predominantly white and male. Despite their numbers in the general population, individuals from subordinate racialized groups make up only five per cent of Canada's legal profession, Aboriginals 0.8 per cent, women 30 per cent and people with disabilities an indiscernibly small number." [17]

Noting that "wage differentials between white lawyers and those from subordinate racialized communities are quite dramatic," the CBA concludes "individuals from these communities may understandably be reluctant to accumulate significant debts, even if provided with increases in financial aid."[18] In short, they may be deterred from going to law school in the first place.

In general, the CBA said, "over 66 per cent of students in the Faculty of Law come from families with incomes above $90,000 per year, as compared to 17 per cent with incomes less than $60,000 per year."[19] In the overall university population, the CBA was concerned "that 38.7 per cent of youth aged 18 to 21 from wealthy families attended university compared to 18.8 per cent of youth from poorer families, and that post-secondary education threatens to become increasingly divided along class lines. Given the intersections between race and family incomes, these divisions will likely be along the lines of race as well."[20]

A risky thing to do

Medical schools find themselves confronted by the same problems as law faculties, only more so, since studying medicine can be even more costly than reading law. The students themselves make the situation clear. For example, listen to Mario Costa [not his real name], now in his second year of medical school at Montreal's McGill University, who expects his eventual student loan debt to easily top a "scary" $150,000.

"It's a fairly risky thing to do," he said, "because they are sizeable loans and should something happen to me, if for some reason I can't finish my training or otherwise be employed as a physician, I'll have a huge debt and nothing to show for it. So I'm taking a $150,000 risk here."

Costa is obviously both bright and motivated, and has made more of an effort than most to realistically explore his career possibilities.

"Once upon a time, I was going to do a PhD in math, but I realized that math research is actually quite lonely," he said.

"You have a chalkboard and the text book. I took a personality test called the Strong Interest Inventory. It matches you up with people who have similar personalities and their occupations, and who are happy in their occupations. Physician was the second choice. The first was research and development manager, but I thought just research wasn't the best for me, so I'll try physician.

"I'm fairly certain I want to do anesthesiology. I bought a book called *The Ultimate Guide to the Medical Specialties* and read through it, got an idea, talked to people, and anesthesiology really seems like an interesting specialty with lots to offer. I like cardiovascular physiology and that's a big part of anesthesiology. And I'm attracted to the acute nature as well–somebody's actually dying in front of you, and being able to help them."

The impulse to help, however, isn't the only thing in play.

"Debt is definitely a contributing factor," he added. "For example, another specialty I was thinking about is physiatry, physical medicine and rehabilitation. They actually make less than family doctors, despite being a five-year [in school] specialty. Physiatrists and psychiatrists both make less than family doctors. The issue is essentially that to do the work that physiatrists and psychiatrists do, they spend a lot of time with their patients. A family doctor will spend maybe 10, 12 minutes with a patient, whereas a psychiatrist might spend half and hour or an hour. It just depends on how quickly you can get them through the door. Which is unfortunate.

"I'm a little ashamed to admit it, but why would I spend three or four years extra doing something to get paid less, when I'm going to have a mountain of debt?"

Nor is paying his own student debt Costa's sole financial concern.

"I come from a below-average-income, middle class family," he explained. "It's a single-parent family. My father died when I was very young. My mom had a job doing clerical work and has a good pension, but her financial position is not particularly strong. A personal dream of mine would be to one day pay off my mother's mortgage."

In this young man's shoes, who would think differently?

Not James Smart [also not his real name], a 23-year-old first-year med student at McMaster University in Hamilton, Ontario, who already owed $30-36,000 in loan debt when he received his bachelor's degree, and expects that to mushroom well past $180,000 when he finishes medical school in three years. "That's about the price of a house where I come from," he said. "I just pretend it doesn't exist. I try to remind myself it's an investment."

His reasoning is a bit different than Costa's, but based on the same imperatives:

"In terms of specialty, I'm looking at going into something that's shorter, because you can pay the debt off quicker." He plans to go into family medicine, even though it may pay less overall, because it requires less time. In the higher-paid specialties, he explained, "you're a resident for longer. So in family medicine you're making money sooner.

"The other thing, I think I'd be more likely to go to an urban centre, even though I am from a rural area, simply because it tends to be better employment possibilities."

Smart has, in fact, given considerable thought to the urban versus rural practice question.

"My parents have a little farm, north of Winnipeg," he said. "I don't come from an affluent family and do come from a rural area, and I'm already saying I'm probably not going to practice in a rural area, because of the way the system is. And I'm only in first year. There's that necessity to service your debt, before you can work in different areas.

"There are some rural areas where you can make a decent amount of income. However, they're very, very rural, very remote areas far up north.

"And even in the act of going to university, I've moved from a rural area to an urban area. So I've spent four years in an urban setting, and I'll have spent another six years in an urban setting, at least, when I've finished school. That's a very large portion of your life, and by then it's kind of difficult to go back to living in a rural area."

Particularly if you owe the government and the banks more than $180,000.

Evidence of medical student flight away from rural areas and from specialties they perceive as lower-paying is not merely anecdotal. The authors of a 2009 paper published in the journal *Family Medicine*[21] noted that:

"The importance of payment as a factor in career decision making increased with higher debt and with advancing [medical school] training.....

"Students both in Canada and the United States have become accustomed to dealing with mortgage-sized debt upon graduation. Over the last several years there has been an increased awareness of the effect of debt on medical students.....while students' decision making is complicated and linked to multiple variables, it is believed remuneration, and even the health of the economy play a role in the migration away from primary care. Implicit in this belief is the assumption that students see primary care careers as a poor choice for redressing the debt incurred during medical training."[22]

According to the paper, fully 40 per cent of fourth-year medical students "would not choose family medicine because of low financial remuneration."[23]

A year earlier, the Canadian Association of Interns and Residents and the Canadian Federation of Medical Students released a joint statement[24] noting that "The average debt carried by a medical resident is $158,728 with average monthly payments of $1,978..... This kind of financial burden has negative implications for the Canadian health care system:

> "Evidence shows that high levels of resident debt:
> * deters trainees from choosing careers in family medicine where the physician shortage is greatest;
> * medical trainees from rural areas of Canada are less likely to practice in rural areas and under-serviced areas because of debt load."

More recently a census, published in 2011 by the Canadian Medical Association, the College of Family Physicians of Canada and the Royal College of Physicians and Surgeons of Canada, revealed that "nearly a quarter, 24 per cent, of medical students said they planned to choose a specialty with a high earning potential, and 17 per cent said they'd choose a shorter residency program to start paying off their debts sooner."[25]

How the shortage of family physicians impacts the lives of patients--who may have no connection whatsoever with student loans or the university system--was described in a recent first-person *Globe & Mail* article,[26] by a woman who had fractured a vertebra and needed follow-up care after being treated at emergency:

"When the man in the plaid shirt took my registration papers and said 'congratulations, you have a family doctor,' I confess I had to hold back a few tears.

> "I had just spent three hours of my Saturday standing in line with hundreds of other people outside a community centre in the Ottawa suburb of Barrhaven to enroll with a new family medicine clinic that is opening at the end of August.
>
> "The wait was inconsequential compared to my long and frustrating search for someone to provide me with basic primary care.
>
> "When I moved to Ottawa in 2005, leaving behind a wonderful doctor in Burlington, Ont., who had looked after my family for more than a decade, I had no idea how difficult it would be to find someone to replace him.
>
> I spent months searching the Internet, calling doctors' offices and imposing upon friends for the names of their physicians–all to no avail. No one was taking patients. My own husband's doctor refused to take me because his practice was full."[27]

After four years, the author had given up hope, resigned to visiting walk-in clinics, but:

> "Then, I fractured a vertebra. The emergency room physicians insisted that I see my family doctor for follow-up care. And I did not have one. Which meant I had to resume the search...."
>
> "I phoned 84 doctors who were listed as practicing within 10 kilometers of my home. Some of their receptionists were polite. Some were surly. All rejected me."[28]

The article described several more fruitless attempts, and the author's eventual success. It took her six years, and hundreds of phone calls, Internet searches, and personal visits to doctors' offices before, after waiting in the long line mentioned in her first paragraph, she finally found care.

No thanks to Canada's student loans system.

At one time, when the compensation for Canadian doctors was much lower than what doctors earned south of the border, the so-called "brain drain" of medical personnel to the United States was also a significant problem. At its nadir in the mid-1990s, as much as half of the graduating classes of some Canadian medical schools moved to the U.S. to practice. The situation was somewhat ameliorated when Canadian doctors' salaries and health care funding generally began to climb again in the following decade, and in 2004 the 30-year-long out-migration of doctors was finally reversed. In that year, 262 physicians left the country, while 317 returned, for a modest net gain of 55 doctors.[29]

But the temptation to move south is still a factor for some medical graduates, as well as for many nursing graduates. As student James Smart, quoted earlier, commented: "A lot of salaries [U.S./Canada] are almost on par now, but the big difference would be in tax rates. I know a medical resident who is training in Canada but very adamantly plans to go to the States, because he's done the math and he can make more money and pay less taxes. I think there's [still] a fair number of McMaster grads that do go to the States."

Nursing graduates don't spend as long in school or face as many fees and extra costs as medical students, but they too feel a financially-inspired wanderlust. As with doctors, nurse out-migration to the U.S. was highest in the 1990s, when government health budgets were being slashed and opportunities for well-paid, full-time nursing work here decreased sharply. In 1995, "the total outflow of RNs to the United States was equivalent to more than a quarter of the 3,000 new RN graduates," a report in *Health Services Research* recalled. "From 1993 to 1994, 40 per cent of the graduates of

Canadian nursing schools from registered nursing educational programs left for the United States."[30]

The figures are no longer as disastrous, but the problem persists, as does a chronic nursing shortage--and the future could hold more trouble. "Canada is projecting a significant registered nurse shortage in the near future, with a shortfall of over 100,000 by 2016," the *Health Services Research* article warned.[31]

Noting that "the ratio of nurses to Canadians remains lower now than in the early 1990s," the Canadian Federation of Nurses Unions advised in 2011 that provincial "premiers should heed the experience of the 1990s, when deep cuts to nursing were a key factor in bed closures, wait times and brain drain to the U.S. Cutting nurses cuts care. It is short term budget gain for long-term pain."[32]

Migration to greener pastures, where pay is better and student loans can be cleared more quickly doesn't necessarily mean moving to the U.S., either. It can mean migration to provinces within Canada where prospects appear better. A May 2009 Statistics Canada fact sheet stated that geographical mobility of health graduates "was highest among graduates in medicine (25 per cent)," and added that "Alberta was the only province with net inflows of both students and graduates."[33]

"Canadians do not want to hear that someone who lives in one province pays less than them for the same life-saving medicines, or that more home care services are provided for free somewhere else, or that it would be faster to get a long-term care bed if they lived in a different province than their own," said the Canadian Federation of Nurses Unions. "We need pan-Canadian solutions to these gaps."[34]

Lack of diversity

Choice of specialty and location of practice after graduation aren't the only things affected by the high cost of medical school. Just as it has proven to be in law schools, the incoming composition of medical school classes is becoming increasingly homogenous.

Tom Perkins [not his real name], in his second year at the University of Ottawa medical school, commented on his classmates' backgrounds:

"Most of the people I know didn't come into medical school with any [undergraduate] debt. Most of them, their parents paid. I'd say the majority are from affluent families. There's not a whole lot that did have government loans. As an undergraduate, they were paying between $12,000 and $13,000 a year. But in medical school you're talking $40,000 to $50,000 a year, and few still have parental support."f

His empirical observations are backed by others:

"Several surveys have concluded that the magnitude of student debt is now affecting who applies to medical school and what areas of practice they choose," said a 2011 policy statement by the British Columbia Medical Association. "The increasing cost of Canadian medical school tuition over the past two decades has resulted in a higher proportion of medical students who come from families with much higher household incomes than the average Canadian, creating issues of equity and accessibility."[35]

"Resident debt creates financial barriers that can limit access to a medical education," said the Canadian Association of Interns and Residents and the Canadian Federation of Medical Students. "This creates a medical workforce with a lack of diversity with respect to economic and cultural background, as often only the wealthiest Canadians can even imagine taking on such debt."[36]

Sadly, even outside of the so-called professional schools like Law and Medicine, it's sometimes only the better-off who consider going to graduate school at all. Mike, for example, is a *cum laud* Ontario engineering graduate who gained top marks while earning his bachelor's degree. His professors urged him to go on, at least for his master's, and he probably could have qualified for some scholarships. But when he added up the debt he'd already accumulated, subtracted the scholarship possibilities, and looked at the bottom line, he gave up on the idea. Today, he manages a Subway fast food outlet in a major Ontario city, and struggles to pay off his undergraduate debt.

Gary S., on the other hand, hasn't yet gone to university, and may never do so. A first-generation Canadian, whose parents immigrated here from the UK, he has a strong interest in writing and in film.

"I used to write poetry, song lyrics, stories," he said. "I write my own philosophy, that kind of stuff. When I was in high school, one of my poems was published. A lot of people tell me, go to school, become a writer. At university, I'd probably get into things like political science, human rights. I was thinking of journalism, and video editing, documentary film. I want to go to college or university, but I'm just putting it off because I'm not looking forward to the debt, and also the crazy amount of stress it [debt] causes.

"Everyone I know who is in school has to work either one or two jobs, basically work full time and go to school, because, you know, the loans don't cover everything. I'd have to have more than one credit card, and whatever else. I'm very good with my money. I have my father to thank for that. I currently have $100 owing on one credit card, and that's it. Debt is a form of slavery, and that's why I'm afraid to get into it."

But he is frustrated. He works as a porter, "stuck in a job where I can't move up" and, where university is concerned, is coming to understand only too well the meaning of the expression "damned if you do, damned if you don't."

How many are like him in Canada? No one can say. There are no surveys of those who aren't there.

The high cost of university or college tuition would likely deter most secondary school graduates, if it weren't for the fact that a university degree or community college diploma is now seen as a basic prerequisite for stable, decently-paid employment. A bachelor's has become the equivalent of yesterday's high school diploma.

Referring to the situation in the U.S., an article posted on the career advice website The Ladders put it succinctly:

"Bruce Hurwitz, president and CEO of Hurwitz Strategic Staffing, said he sees this issue come up regularly. 'Every time I have tried to get a client to waive the college degree requirement in light of a candidate's exemplary work experience, I have been refused,' he said. 'They almost always say that it is their policy that all employees have at least a college degree.'

"Such jobs now account for most of the economy. Nearly 60 per cent of American jobs now require at least a bachelor's degree according to 'Help Wanted: Projections of jobs and education requirements through 2018,' a June 2010 report released by the Centre on Education and the Workforce at Georgetown University. That number jumped from 28 per cent in 1973 to 59 per cent in 2008 and is expected to rise to 63 per cent over the next decade, the report said."[37]

Secondary school students in Canada are well aware of this, as the most recent figures for Ontario demonstrate:

"High school students continue to apply to Ontario universities in record numbers, continuing an 11-year trend of increasing demand for university education, according to the Council of Ontario Universities (COU).

"The total number of first-year applicants rose by 2.2 per cent to 90,373 applicants at the January 11 deadline for secondary school applicants, while the number of applications they made [to more than one university] rose by 2.4 per cent, to 392,742 according to statistics collected from the Ontario Universities Application Centre."[38]

"Damned if they do, damned if they don't," "caught between a rock and a hard place," "between the frying pan and the fire": the choices presented to young people in Canada have become a set of clichés. The prime consideration in opting for post-secondary school is no longer talent, ability, interest, desire, or even the good of society, but--plainly and simply--money.

Other impacts
The student loan system, and high tuition rates that compound its effects, have still other impacts on society, exacerbating an already-burgeoning trend toward privatization of all government services and functions, and the creation of what some have called a "shadow government," or "shadow civil service."

Perhaps worse than this, they've also contributed to the adoption by the academic world and its administrators of an increasingly commercial, mercantile attitude towards the pursuit of knowledge. What was once seen as learning for its own sake, or for the good of society, has come more and more to be viewed as a simple monetary transaction. Knowledge is something to be hoarded, bought and sold as a commodity. Universities sell knowledge "products," and students buy them, so that later on they can sell themselves on the job market as still another "product."

A university degree is reduced to a mere credential for marketing purposes--in this case the marketing of human beings to corporate recruiters.

In such an intellectual environment, old-fashioned notions like academic freedom, independent thinking, pure research for the sake of advancing the frontiers of a discipline, regardless of the presence or absence of immediate, practical applications–all go by the boards.

Strapped for funds by the loss of government support, universities not only raise their price to students, but go looking hungrily for new sources of income. Corporate donors become the new Big Men on Campus, and their support can come not with strings, but chains attached.

Research funds are available only for projects that will return a fast, or moderately fast profit, either for the university itself, for its corporate donors, or both. Faculty members who become troublesome, by nosing into research areas that donors find uncomfortable, find their projects aren't approved. Those who wish to share their work–seen now by universities and donors alike as "proprietary"--too widely with fellow scientists or academics, find themselves shunted aside, in some cases forced right out of their jobs.

Meanwhile, those academics who enthusiastically join the march to profit prosper along with the money lenders. In some cases, as will be seen shortly, they actually *are* the money lenders, or collectors or administrators.

The knock-on effects of a for-profit, privatized Academe, locked directly or indirectly into the loans industry, are legion. But more on that in a later chapter. It's time now to take a look at the folks who are running the show, the government and financial sector players responsible for the Canadian student loan system as it is today.

1. Tracey Tyler, "Access to justice a 'basic right,'" *The Toronto Star*, 12 August 2007, as posted online on http://www.thestar.com/printarticle/245548

2. Robert Todd, "Legal Aid: a system in peril," *The Canadian Lawyer*, October 2010, as posted online at http://www.canadianlawyermag.com/Legal-aid-a-system-in-peril.html?...

3. Michael Lewis, "Drawing a clear line," *The Canadian Bar Association*, Pro bono RISING, as posted online at http://www.cba.org/cba/national/augsep04/PrintHtml.aspx?DocId=6224

4. Todd, *Op. Cit.*

5. Tyler, *Op. Cit.*

6. *The Canadian Press*, "Children need legal help, advocate says," 4 May 2011, as posted online by *Canadian Broadcasting Corporation (CBC)*, http://www.cbc.ca/news/canada/saskatchewan/story/2011/05/04/sk-pr...

7. Tracey Tyler, "Cuts to Legal Aid hit families hard," *The Toronto Star*, 12 March 2007, as posted online at Pro Bono Law Ontario, http://www.pblo.org/news/article.135197-Cuts_to_legal_ais_hit_famil...

8. *Ibid.*

9. Todd, *Op. Cit.*

10. Canadian Bar Association, "Response to the Provost Study of Accessibility and Career Choice in the University of Toronto Faculty of Law, April 2003, 15.

11. Shirley Neuman, "Provost Study of Accessibility and Career Choice in the Faculty of Law," 24 February 2003, University of Toronto.

12. Canadian Bar Association, *Op. Cit.*.

13. *Op. Cit.*, 6.

14. *Op. Cit.*, 10.

15. *Op. Cit.*, 1.

16. *Op. Cit.*, 2-3.

17. *Op. Cit.*, 3.

18. *Op. Cit.*, 5.

19. *Op. Cit.*, 13.

20. *Loc. Cit.*

21. Dante J. Morra, Glenn Regehr and Shipra Ginsburg, "Medical Students, Money and Career Selection: Students' perception of financial factors and remuneration in family medicine," *Family Medicine*, 2009; 41(2): 105-10.

22. *Op. Cit.*, 105.

23. *Op. Cit.*, 107.

24. CNW Newswire, Canadian Association of Interns and Residents, "Changes to Canada Student Loans Program don't help medical residents or the doctor shortage," 27 August 2008, as posted online at http://www.newswire.ca/en/story/251029/changes-to-canada-student-l...

25. CBC News, "Debt woes weigh on future doctors' plans," 28 September 2011, as posted online at http://www.cbc.ca/news/health/story/2011/09/28/physician-survey-debt...

26. Gloria Galloway, "The soul-destroying search for a family doctor," *The Globe & Mail*, 21 August 2011, as posted online at http://www.theglobeandmail.com/life/health/new-health/health-policy/t...

27. *Loc. Cit.*

28. *Loc. Cit.*

29. The Canadian Press, "Canada's brain drain trend reverses for doctors: report," 12 October 2006, as posted online at http://www.cbc.ca/news/health/story/2006/10/12/doctors-migrate.html

30. Lisa Little, "Nurse Migration: a Canadian case study," *Health Services Research*, June 2007, 42(3 Pt. 2), 1336-1353.

31. *Op. Cit.*, 1336.

32. Canadian Federation of Nurses Unions, "Nurses call on premiers to find pan-Canadian solutions to public health care: united front will be needed to engage federal government," 20 July 2011, as posted online at: http://www.nursesunions.ca/news/nurses-call-premiers-find-pan-canad...

33. Statistics Canada, "Where do health university graduates move after graduation?" May 2009, Fact Sheet No. 2, Health Human Resources and Education in Canada, Catalogue No. 81-600-X--Issue No. 002.

34. Canadian Federation of Nurses Unions, *Op. Cit.*

35. British Columbia Medical Association, Policy Statement, "Medical student and resident debt relief," August 2011, as posted online at http://www.bcma.org

36. CNW Newswire, Canadian Association of Interns and Residents, *Op. Cit.*

37. Debra Donston-Miller, "Finding a job without a college degree," *The Ladders*, 9 August 2010, http://www.theladders.com/career-advice/finding-job-without-college...

38. CNW Newswire, Council of Ontario Universities, "Strong rise in number of university applications and applicants across Ontario," 16 January 2012, as posted online at http://www.newswire.ca/en/story/906205/strong-rise-in-number-of-un...

Chapter Six: Who's (who) on First

*"By two-headed Janus,
nature has framed strange fellows in her time."*

–Shakespeare, *The Merchant of Venice*

Ottawa's traditionally leading political players, both Tory and Liberal (but not, for the most part, New Democrats), have long enjoyed good relations with the Canadian banking industry. Former Prime Minister Brian Mulroney, before entering politics, was in the business himself, as Stevie Cameron wrote in 1995:

"The Canadian Imperial Bank of Commerce has been the Tory party's bank for many years, and it too has had especially close ties with Brian Mulroney, who served on its board before entering politics. (Today, the CIBC holds the mortgage on the Mulroney house in Montreal."[1]

Liberal Prime Minister Jean Chretien, when he left politics, took a seat on the board of the Toronto-Dominion Bank.[2] In the 1993 election that brought his Grits to power, ending a nearly decade-long Tory era, the 13 largest contributors to the federal Liberal campaign were banks and other financial corporations, including "Bank of Montreal, Royal Bank, RBC Dominion Securities Inc., Canadian Imperial Bank of Commerce, Toronto-Dominion Securities, Toronto-Dominion Bank, and the Bank of Nova Scotia."[3]

Up until 2006, when federal campaign finance regulations were radically altered, the country's banks showed consistent largesse, year-in-year-out, contributing millions to both federal parties, but next to nothing to the NDP. The Parliament of Canada website, for example, shows under Political Contributions that, from 1982 to 2003, Canada's six largest banks showered multimillions of dollars on the Liberal, Progressive Conservative and Reform parties, but only a paltry $28,200 on the NDP ($20,000 in 1999, $7,000 in 1998, $800 in 1995 and $400 in 1992).[4]

The story for most provincial parties, with the exception of years when the NDP has governed in, for example, Saskatchewan or Ontario (under the now-very-Liberal Bob Ray), has been similar. Quebec is its own, typically atypical case.

Since the Federal Accountability Act was passed in 2006, it has been illegal for corporations—including banks—or unions, to directly contribute funds to a federal political party or candidate. However, individuals—including all of the board members, officers and employees of corporations—can contribute up to $1,200 apiece, if they like. And there are many other ways to boost a federal party or candidate. In 2012, for example, a minor scandal ensured when a private fundraising event was set up where individuals with ties to radio broadcasting businesses contributed money to a Conservative MP connected to the minister who oversaw the Canadian Radio-television and Telecommunications Commission, which regulates radio.

The campaign finance rules in several provinces still permit direct corporate and union donations to provincial parties and candidates.

There is nothing improper in any of this, of course. It only puts things in their overall context.

It should also be noted that, during the recent bank-induced financial disasters in the U.S. and worldwide, where credit-bubbling bankers were cast in a less-than-ideal light, Canada's banks came off smelling like roses in comparison. Veritable models of probity and responsibility.

That said, it should also be noted that our nation's bankers are not necessarily all, or always, saints.

For example, the notorious Enron scandal back in 2003 managed to ensnare the CIBC. The U.S. Securities and Exchange Commission (SEC) fined the bank US$ 80 million for its role in manipulation of Enron financial statements. The amount included "$37.5 million to repay ill-gotten gains, a $37.5 million penalty and $5 million in interest."[5] The SEC also sued three CIBC officers, Executive Vice President Daniel Ferguson, Executive Director Mark Wolf and Ian Schottlaender, former managing director of CIBC's finance group in New York. All three settled, paying hefty damages in return for an agreement that they neither admit nor deny wrongdoing. Schottlaender was also barred for five years from swerving as an officer or director of any publicly traded company.[6]

The SEC complaint charged "CIBC and the three executives with having helped Enron to mislead its investors through a series of complex structured finance transactions over a period of years preceding Enron's bankruptcy."[7]

In 2004, the CIBC settled a class action suit on behalf of VISA cardholders, who had claimed that conversion by the bank of foreign currency transactions had resulted in an undisclosed or inadequately disclosed mark-up. In exchange for not having to admit liability and to avoid further litigation, the bank paid cardholders $13.85 million, the United Way $1 million, the Class Action Fund of the Law Society of Upper Canada $1.65 million and $3 million in legal fees.[8]

That same year, CIBC also announced it would refund $24 million to some of its customers in connection with erroneous overdraft and mortgage charges, discovered in the course of an internal review. "This is being done as part of CIBC's effort to correct its error and to ensure that it distributes to customers all of the money it received in error," the bank said.[9]

The Enron debacle pursued the bank into 2005, when CIBC paid $2.4 billion to settle another class action suit brought by a group of pension funds and investment managers, including the University of California, who claimed that "systematic fraud by Enron and its officers led to the loss of billions and the collapse of the company."[10]

The bank also agreed to pay US$125 million to settle its part in the 2003 Mutual fund scandal, in which the SEC alleged fund customers' "boosted trading profits at the expense of long-term mutual fund shareholders." Under the settlement CIBC neither admitted nor denied the allegations.[11]

That same unlucky year of 2005, CIBC was also criticized by the Privacy Commissioner of Canada for the way it dealt with "incidents involving the bank misdirecting faxes containing customers' personal information:

"One involved misdirecting faxes to a scrapyard operator in West Virginia from 2001 to 2004. The misdirected faxes contained the social security numbers, home addresses, phone numbers and detailed bank account data of several hundred bank customers.

".... in both cases, the commissioner noted that the bank did not inform the affected clients, whose personal information was compromised, until the incidents became public and an investigation was underway.

"A few days after the story broke on CTV News and in the Globe & Mail, CIBC announced that it had banned its employees from using fax machines to transmit any documents containing confidential customer information."[12]

Nor has CIBC been the only Canadian bank struck, indirectly, by such misfortune. The year this book was written, in 2012, TD Bank, the U.S. arm of the TD Financial Group, was ordered by a federal jury in Florida to pay a Texas-based group of investors, Coquina Investment, $32 million in compensatory damages and $35 million in punitive damages over the role it played in a $1.2 billion Ponzi scheme. The scheme was set up by U.S. lawyer Scott Rothstein, subsequently disbarred and now serving a prison sentence.[13]

According to the Toronto *Star*, Coquina's complaint and court testimony showed:

"Rothstein used the TD Bank to provide bank records, account balances, verifications, often arranging meetings in the conference room of a branch.

"Frank Spinosa, the bank's regional vice-president, met with Coquina investors in person and had telephone conversations with them, which 'contributed to this aura of legitimacy,' the complaint said.

"Spinosa was called to testify, but asserted his Fifth Amendment right not to incriminate himself at least 160 times. The bank said he has not been an employee for two years."[14]

All of which goes to show that large institutions, dealing with large sums of money, sometimes slip.

It does not show that banks in general, particularly Canadian banks, are as a rule untrustworthy, incompetent or dishonest. Much less criminal. To be criminal, any business that lends money would have to violate the *Criminal Code* of

Canada, which devotes considerable space to defining what is not permitted in money lending.

For example, Section 347 of the Code, "Criminal Interest Rate," defines a criminal rate as "an effective annual rate of interest calculated in accordance with generally accepted actuarial practices and principles that exceeds 60 per cent on the credit advanced under an agreement or arrangement."[15]

It adds that:

"Interest means the aggregate of all charges and expenses, whether in the form of a fee, fine, penalty, commission or other similar charge or expense or in any other form, paid or payable, for the advancing of credit under an agreement or arrangement, by or on behalf of the person to whom the credit is or is to be advanced, irrespective of the person to whom any such charges and expenses are or are to be paid or payable....."[16]

Sixty per cent or more, and you're officially dealing with a crook. Less than 60 and you are dealing with a business that sells a product to the public. James Scurlock, in his best-selling book *Maxed Out*,[17] describes that product concisely:

".... banking is about selling a single product: debt. That product can be packaged a million different ways–car loans, mortgages, lines of credit, overdraft protection, credit cards, cell phones, etc., etc.–but, in the end, the product is an obligation to be repaid, with interest. And the price of that product is however much interest and fees can be charged on the original amount. **The more interest and fees a bank can charge, the more profitable the product** *[bold face not in original]."*[18]

Students, teachers, politicians, the general public, and perhaps most of all parents, should keep that fact in mind when assessing the wisdom of financing the education and training of young Canadians, or older Canadians returning to school to upgrade their qualifications, via the mechanism of student loans.

Things changed
As noted in Chapter One, prior to the mid-1980s Canada's post-secondary school system was reasonably stable, mainly publicly-funded, and characterized by relatively low tuition fees and student aid offered chiefly in the form of grants.

Then things changed.

First under Mulroney's Tories and then Chretien's Liberals, federal transfer payments to the provinces, which under the division of powers of Canadian Confederation constituted the federal government's mechanism of support for education, were repeatedly slashed. So were provincial government education budgets. With less and less cash coming from government, colleges and universities had no choice but to raise tuition. The price of going to school doubled, and doubled again. At the same time, the amount of provincial government grants available to students with assessed needs was cut back massively. From 1990 to 1995 alone, provincial grants fell from $305.14 million to $48.36 million–a drop of 84 per cent.[19]

According to researchers funded by the C.D. Howe Institute:

"As late as the 1990/91 academic year, almost all provinces gave needy students some form of grants or bursaries (the structure and generosity varied). By 1994/95, most of these aid packages had been eliminated, leaving behind only a scattering of grant programs aimed at fairly narrow subgroups of the student population."[20]

Students whose families were not independently wealthy were pinched more and more tightly, leaving no alternative but to borrow to pay for their courses.

The price of knowledge became debt.

The system changed in other ways as well. From 1964, when the Canada Student Loans Program (CSLP) was instituted, to 1995, federal student loans were granted and administered by private banks, but guaranteed 100 per cent against default by the federal government. The CSLP paid the interest on the loan while a student was in school, and for six months after graduation. If a borrower defaulted, Ottawa "paid the bank [both the principal and accumulated interest], took over responsibility for the loan and attempted to recover the unpaid balance, usually by employing a private collection agency."[21]

After 1995, private banks continued to grant and administer loans, but also accepted responsibility "for the risk of default, in return for a government payment of five per cent of the value of the loans going into repayment."[22] Under this "risk share" bargain, which was to run until 2000, the banks would take the government payment, but could also attempt on their own to recover the unpaid balances, either using their own staff or by employing a collection agency.

The banks still seemed to have a relatively good thing going, but apparently didn't think it was as good as the pre-1995 deal, when 100 per cent of defaults were absorbed by the government. Bank complaints about defaults, which some observers thought were exaggerated, grew, and in 1997 the federal government amended the Bankruptcy and Insolvency Act to prohibit student loan debtors who fell on hard times from including their student loan debts in bankruptcy. Student debts became non-dischargeable in bankruptcy for two years following graduation. Less than a year later, in June 1998, the term during which student loans could not be discharged by bankruptcy was extended to 10 years. The federal New Democrats tried in 2005 to reduce the term back to two years, as did the Senate in 2007, but to no avail. This bankruptcy exclusion followed the U.S. example, where federally-backed student loans had been non-dischargeable in bankruptcy since 1976 (all U.S. student loans, including those not backed by government, were declared non-dischargeable in 2005). Amendments to the 1998 U.S. Higher Education Act had also eliminated all statutes of limitations for the collection of student loans, and specifically exempted such loans from state usury laws. Student borrowers were also excluded from coverage by the Truth in Lending Act, and from the Fair Debt Collection and Practices Act, although, paradoxically, collection agents are still subject to the latter.

U.S. students were declared, in effect, a kind of outlaw, second class category of persons who, once in debt for whatever amount, became fair game for anything. It was open season on them. The existence of a variety of debt dispute, loan consolidation and rehabilitation programs administered by the U.S. Department of Education seemed only to complicate matters.

Some thought the same thing was starting to happen to Canadian students, when they were singled out, alone among their fellow citizens, to lose their right to financial relief via bankruptcy if they fell on hard times (an effort was made to challenge this in court, on grounds that it violated the Canadian Charter of Rights, but in June 2005 Ontario Superior Court Justice Gordon Sedgwick ruled against it).

Observers would become even more certain that Canada was going the way of the USA in 2009, when the federal bank act was amended (see below).

In 2000, yet more things shifted. The "risk-share" arrangement between Ottawa and participating banks ended, cutting off the banks' five per cent fee, and the Canada Student Financial Assistance Act was amended to permit the federal government to finance its student loans directly. After August 1, 2000, the Government of Canada financed all new federal loans, via the newly-established National Student Loans Service Centre (NSLSC). Ottawa would contribute 60 per cent of a borrower's loan funds, while the provinces and territories (except for Quebec, Nunavut and the Northwest Territories which didn't participate) supplied the remaining 40 per cent.

Private banks could still issue separate lines of credit to students on their own, and did, but loans granted under the formal aegis of the Canada Student Loans Program were henceforth given directly by federal and provincial governments, from government coffers.

According to some sources, at this time defaulted loans were intended to be assigned for collection to the Canada Revenue Agency (CRA). However, existing contracts awarded by the NSLSC's parent federal ministry, Human Resources and Skills Development Canada, may not yet have run out. According to a CRA press officer, default collection remained with the ministry until August 2005, when:

"... the responsibility for the collection of defaulted Canada Student Loans was transferred from HRSDC to the CRA, including the responsibility for the management of private collection agencies assisting in the recovery of defaulted Canada Student Loans. Since June 2009, the CRA stopped using the services of the private collection agencies and the collection of defaulted Canada Student Loans is done by CRA employees only."[23]

As for the administration of *non*-defaulted loans by the newly-minted NSLSC, this was not given to Canada Revenue Agency, but instead directly to private, third party "providers." Initially, there were two. The Canadian Imperial Bank of Commerce, via its subsidiary Edulinx Canada Corp. (created by the bank in 1999), was contracted to administer borrowers attending public post-secondary institutions, while another, independent company handled borrowers attending private institutions.

The correct name of this second firm at the time is unclear. According to the website of the federal ministry responsible for student loans, Human Resources and Skills Development Canada (HRSDC), "Resolve Corporation" held the contract beginning in 2000.[24] However, other records indicate that Resolve's parent company, First Service Corp., created Resolve–formerly known as BDP Business Data Services Ltd.– by merging four units in the First Service business services division, in May 2004.[25]

Whatever the name at the time, eventually loans for students at private institutions were handled by Resolve.

Subsequent to 2000, the names and responsibilities of the various private "service providers" contracted by governments to handle student loans becomes a bit confusing. Responsibility shifted back and forth, from one company to another, while the companies themselves changed ownership or changed names. Some companies held contracts with both the federal NSLSC and provincial governments at the same time. Others didn't. To anyone not used to observing corporate mergers and acquisitions, keeping track of them sometimes seems like keeping track of which walnut shell the pea is under.

But the actions of some of these companies--or their parent firms, which in some cases were American rather than Canadian--weren't always exemplary. As in the movies, it's important to get the cast, and where possible the timelines, straight.

In 1999, as noted above, CIBC created Edulinx, at least partly with staff from its own call centres, to handle the administration of student loans. In 2001, a Toronto-based company called Repayassist Canada Corp. was re-baptized Tricura Canada Inc., and not long afterward Tricura was acquired by Edulinx, becoming its wholly-owned subsidiary. Students who phoned the NSLSC call centre began getting operators who responded either "National Student Loans Service Centre," or "Edulinx," or "Tricura."

Unless they were studying at a private college, in which case they might hear either "NSLSC" or "Resolve."

Then the pea shifted to a different shell. CIBC decided to cut back its involvement in the student loans system, and in December 2004 sold Edulinx and its Tricura subsidiary to a company called Nelnet Canada, which was itself a subsidiary of a much larger American company, Nelnet Inc. The American firm had originally been called UNIPAC Loan Service Corp., but was re-branded with the Nelnet moniker in 1996.

Why CIBC decided to sell Edulinx is uncertain. Not long after the 1995 switch to risk sharing, CIBC began reducing its involvement in the administration of provincial government student loans. Citing high bankruptcy rates (despite the two- and 10-years bans imposed on student loan bankruptcy), it had pulled out of Nova Scotia in 1997 and Manitoba in 1998.

But that was six years earlier. By 2004, Edulinx employed some 600 people and was "the largest servicer of government sponsored student loans in Canada."[26]

In a news release reporting its fourth quarter 2005 financial statements, CIBC noted that its "non-interest expenses" had been "partially offset by lower operational losses and lower expenses due to the Edulinx sale."[27]

Chorus of complaint

Prior to the sale, Edulinx, Tricura and the NSLSC had been the target of a steady chorus of customer dissatisfaction, which by 2004 had become a veritable storm of complaint. Stories in the press, and posting after posting on Mark O'Meara's CanadaStudentDebt, and other student loan websites, told of "serious service quality issues and, in some cases defaults due to lost documentation, underestimated documentation volumes, fax machines that did not function properly, and poorly trained staff."[28]

The Canadian Press quoted Judy Dyck, president of the Canadian Association of Student Financial Aid Administrators, in an April 2004 story:

"Customer service has gone downhill since Ottawa took over the [student loan] program, [Dyck] said from her University of Winnipeg office.

"Problems are most intense in September and January when university and college terms begin, she said.

"Financial aid officers are often 'stuck with crying, very upset students in their offices who are desperately waiting for money for rent, food and the basics of life.

"'And then when one calls to figure out what the problem is, every time you have to begin with a new person and start the story all over again. You'll get a request for slightly different documentation than...the previous time. You send that in, and there's still a delay.'

"Lack of training for student loan operators seems to be a major problem, Dyck said.

"If they're not 100 per cent trained and 100 per cent clear, they start confusing the students incredibly.'"[29]

The story added:

"A former Edulinx worker said operators are pressured to handle as many as 11 calls per hour, allowing less than six minutes per call. That leaves little time for note-taking or complete service, said the ex-employee, who spoke on condition of anonymity."[30]

Other press reports were equally critical:
"..... difficulties in dealing with Edulinx or the NSLSC. Horror stories from universities across the entire country detail accounts of lost forms, accrued interest and incompetent staff. It's just a nuisance for some, but other students can find themselves forced out of school prematurely. University graduates who find work watch as their salaries are eaten up by loan payments. Government programs that exist to ease the burden of repayment, such as interest relief, operate under such strict guidelines that many who should qualify for assistance do not.

"..... The most common forms lost are confirmation of enrolment forms, which notify the NSLSC or Edulinx of a student's continued enrolment, thereby preventing any interest from accruing on their existing loans. The other forms most frequently lost are interest relief application forms, designed to provide relief for recent graduates who cannot afford to pay off their student loans once their loans enter repayment.....

""When forms are lost, interest begins to accumulate on the account. Before a new confirmation of enrolment or interest relief form can be accepted by the NSLSC, any accumulated interest must be paid off. Students, many of whom live on tight *budgets, can be forced out of school because they can't afford the payments.*"[31]

Various in-house surveys of borrower satisfaction with NSLSC service had indicated that roughly 70 per cent of customers were satisfied. O'Meara pointed out, however, that "in most financial sectors, this [30 per cent *dissatisfied*] rate would be unacceptable. Further investigation reveals that those surveyed were mostly new borrowers, while only a minority were actually in repayment when they were being surveyed."[32] Other critics noted that the survey questions were too general and didn't focus on chronic problems, such as interest rates or lost paperwork. What such surveys really showed, they said, was that a sizeable chunk of student borrowers were upset with the service even before they started repaying their loans. The rate among borrowers in general might have been much higher.

O'Meara added that his website, where trouble with the system was the subject, received between 1,000 and 3,000 hits per week.

Numerous complaints about the situation had been forwarded to CIBC's head office in Toronto in January 2003, with copies for Chairman and CEO John Hunkin and other senior bank officers. Prominent in the complaints were repeated claims that the bank lost, or denied having received, documents required to qualify for interest relief, or to maintain a borrower's status as a full-time student exempt from interest accrual.

A brief reply from CIBC Customer Care Manager Clarence Layne referred O'Meara to the bank's Customer Care telephone number, and enclosed a brochure. Said Layne, in an oddly ungrammatical paragraph: "Mr. O'Meara, I acknowledge that our response fully address the concerns you have raised. However, we appreciate the feedback and will ensure that it is passed to the appropriate are for review."

In 2004, students found out where the CIBC president was staying during the annual shareholders meeting and flooded his hotel room with telephone messages to "please fix the student loan system."

O'Meara also gathered a bundle of student complaints from his website, together with numerous press clippings, and forwarded them to then Prime Minister Paul Martin, to the Liberal government's then-HRSDC Minister, Joe Volpe, Social Development Minister Ken Dryden, the Auditor General, and to the leaders and education critics for the opposition Conservatives and NDP.

O'Meara recalls: "The general response from the government at the time was 'talk to your bank.' But when we said the bank directed us to talk to the collection agency and wouldn't talk to us, the government official quietly said 'sorry, I don't know what to say, we're told to say that.'"

Such a tepid response was not surprising, given what government priorities in the area of consumer protection seemed to be at the time. A 2003 *National Post* article reported the results of a study by Ontario's provincial auditor, of inspections performed by the Ministry of Consumer and Business Services:

"Ontario government investigators had a single-minded focus on inspecting adult video stores while ignoring thousands of consumer complaints about collection agencies and motor vehicle repairs, Ontario's provincial auditor said yesterday.

"The Auditor found the Ministry of Consumer and Business Services carried out almost 1,600 inspections of video retail stores, about which it had received eight complaints.

"However, there were about 4,000 complaints and inquiries related to debt collectors last year, for which the ministry conducted 10 inspections. And almost 2,000 complaints about motor vehicle repairs brought about six inspections...... the ministry devoted over 95 per cent of its inspection resources to inspecting this [video retailer] industry."

The story added that *"90 per cent of callers from outside Toronto to the office's main call centre got a busy signal."*[33]

First things first.

O'Meara's complaint package to the government was accompanied by a cover letter, listing "common problems with the student loan program." The list was lengthy, but worth quoting in detail:

> "* People who need help do not qualify for interest relief or debt reduction. A person with over $60,000 in student loans would be disqualified from interest relief if their gross income is $35,000 per year, even though that would be a 50 per cent debt ratio! With $25,000 in student loans, you'd be disqualified at $26,000 gross income per year;
> "* No statement of principal, interest and payments, and outstanding balance, is available to borrowers. If you ask for one, you are out of luck! You are expected to accept the number they quote [verbally, by phone] without any proof;
> "* Edulinx and the bank lose interest relief and continuation of enrolment forms, resulting in defaults and destroyed credit ratings and harassment;

"* Because of all the program changes, students graduate with up to six different loans, each managed by a different organization;
"* Many low-income people have paid thousands of dollars in interest without reducing any of their principal. The student loan system has become a tax on the working poor;
"* Collection agencies routinely break the law, using illegal harassment and collection techniques;
"* Collection agencies refuse to accept payments and illegally harass clients and their families;
"* People who want to pay their loans can't because HRSDC doesn't know who has the loan;
"* Edulinx and HRDC staff give wrong answers. Student loan legislation is complicated. Staff don't know or understand the regulations;
"* There is no way you can find out what you owe. If you think you've paid off your loan, you may be surprised to find that five years later, they call you and tell you there was another portion that was not paid and you owe it and all the outstanding interest, and your credit rating has been ruined;
"* Presently, PhD students run out of interest free weeks and have to pay back their undergrad loans while they are still full-time students;
"* Graduates are leaving the country because of overwhelming debt, creating a brain drain;
"* If a disability occurs more than seven months after you finish school, no help is available;
"* Because of the changes to the Bankruptcy Act, people are avoiding further education in order to avoid restarting the clock;

"*   Debt loads have reached horribly crippling levels for graduates. Students with no family support end up with huge loans in the range of $40-60,000;
"We beg you to:
"*   Fix the administrative problems of lost forms and misinformation;
"*   Require collection agencies to follow Canadian laws;
"*   Provide interest relief to the people that do not qualify for it, but obviously need it;
"*   Use net income as a determination for interest relief;
"*   Reduce the interest rate on student loans;
"*   Apply tax seizures to the student loan principal, rather than interest;
"*   Provide statements to borrowers."

The question of collection agencies, referred to in the list of complaints, was a key one. Once a loan went into default–and this often seemed to happen, as already mentioned, through NSLSC or its contractors' error–the borrower's file was subcontracted out to these agencies, who earned fees for their services over and above the original loan principal and interest. As noted previously, even the CRA, assigned to handle defaults in 2000, hired private contractors to do it. Not until 2009 was this job assumed completely by "CRA employees."[34]

The agencies' goal was fast turnover and consequent fast profits, and a given agency might hold on to a borrower's file for only a short time before selling it to another agency, for a smaller fee than it would have made if it collected the loan itself. A borrower's file might thus rotate through several agencies, with fees accumulating, and eventually the NSLSC or its service contractors might no longer know who was handling it. The same would be true of provincial governments, or banks that granted lines of credit to students outside of the Canada Student Loan Program.

Conversely, the most recent collection agency handling a file might not be aware that the original loan had been paid off, to the original lender. Even if an agency was aware, it would still be interested in collecting its own fee.

The collection industry is notorious for its freewheeling ways and single-minded focus. Canadian collectors tend to be less extreme than their U.S. counterparts, but not always, and less so if they are owned by a U.S. parent company. Alan Michael Collinge, in his already-mentioned book, *The Student Loan Scam*, describes one American company:

"Premiere Credit of North America, LLC, is a self-styled shark of the student loan collection business. Indeed, Premiere's corporate headquarters houses a 4,000-gallon shark tank in its lobby. The company proudly displays the shark tank on the home page of its corporate website, claiming that these predators have 'qualities that Premiere Credit of North America nurtures as part of its corporate culture.'"[35]

Collinge also quotes Joseph Leal, president of U.S. Recoveries Worldwide, that "student loan collections are like none other. I could write a book on the various illegal activities I have witnessed in this industry. They do things that no other industry could get away with."[36]

But more on collection agencies, and "erroneous" defaults, later in this chapter.

Enter Nelnet, and Sallie Mae

Throughout the history of Canada's student loan system, American companies have played a significant role, although the nature of that role hasn't always been apparent. It becomes interesting when one looks at the names of the directors, officers and staff of the U.S. companies in question, as we will shortly do, and their Canadian connections.

But first, let's complete the story of the evolution of Canada's system.

The company that bought Edulinx/Tricura from the CIBC, Nelnet Canada, was as noted a subsidiary of U.S.-based Nelnet Inc., whose name hit the headlines in the American press in February 2007, when then-New York Attorney General Andrew Cuomo launched a probe of "deceptive lending practices by student loan providers" in the U.S.[37]

The probe was only the first of several in the U.S. to look at Nelnet, Citibank, The College Board, EduCap, and the truly big fish in the American student loan big pond, Sallie Mae (SLM Corporation, formerly the Student Loan Marketing Association). Nelnet's role in the Cuomo investigation involved possible "conflict of interest issues relating to lenders being placed on preferred lender lists at colleges and universities."[38] Investigators looked at agreements or relationships between lender/loan consolidation companies and school officials, as well as alumni groups, that endorsed companies. Nelnet said it had 120 such agreements with alumni groups, all legal under U.S. federal law.[39]

The Cuomo probe's interest in Nelnet concluded when the company "agreed to contribute $2 million to a national fund for educating high school seniors and their parents regarding the financial aid process."[40] and to adopt the attorney general's Code of Conduct.

Nelnet had also been targeted in 2007 by then-Nebraska Attorney General Jon Bruning, in an investigation which had alleged kickbacks, improper inducements, and gifts by loan providers to colleges and universities.[41] The company reached a settlement with Bruning in April 2007, agreeing to "voluntarily adopt a Nelnet student loan Code of Conduct and commit $1 million to help educate students and their families on how to plan and pay for their education."[42] A New America Foundation report later claimed that officials from Nelnet and Union Bank & Trust Company, both owned by the same family, gave $16,100 to Bruning for his U.S. Senate election campaign, including $2,300 from Nelnet President Jeff Noordhoek, "16 days before the two would appear together to announce the $1 million settlement."[43]

Bruning decided in August to forgive the cash obligation "after the company announced it had reached [the] separate $2 million settlement" with Cuomo. A spokesperson for Bruning explained that "it doesn't make sense to create two funds for the same purpose."[44]

Nelnet had been involved in other, bigger controversies--including one that stretched back to 1993 and eventually became known in newspaper headlines as the "9.5 scandal." The scandal, which embroiled several other student loan companies, including Sallie Mae, was first uncovered by a U.S. Department of Education researcher named Jon Oberg.

In the 1980s, a shaky economy and rising loan costs had prompted the U.S. Congress to subsidize non-profit lenders by guaranteeing them a 9.5 per cent return on certain student loans. The economy improved and Congress rescinded the policy in 1993. But lenders, including Nelnet–which was created when Nebraska's non-profit student loan agency converted to for-profit status–devised a strategy to keep the subsidy coming, and growing. According to reports:

"... a group of lenders devised a strategy to aggressively grow the volume of loans that they claimed were eligible for the inflated payments. They did so by transferring loans that qualified for the 9.5 subsidy payment to other financing vehicles and recycling the proceeds into new loans that they claimed

were then eligible for the subsidy.... By repeating the transfer and recycling process over and over, Nelnet increased the amount of loans for which it sought the 9.5 per cent rate from about $550 million in 2003 to nearly $4 billion in 2004."[45]

Oberg helped discover the situation, and in 2003 warned his superiors that the companies were collecting millions in what he believed were improper subsidies. His warnings were largely ignored, until in January 2007, the U.S. Education Department's Inspector General recommended that $278 million in overpayments be recovered from Nelnet. Then-DOE Undersecretary Sara Tucker, however, allowed Nelnet to keep the $278 million, providing it agreed to halt the practice.[46]

In September 2007, Oberg filed a whistleblower lawsuit, on behalf of the U.S. government, against Nelnet and several other defendants, including Sallie Mae subsidiary Southwest Student Services Corporation. The suit demanded that the money earned via the 9.5 payments–estimated at nearly $1 billion--be returned to the government. In August 2010, Nelnet agreed to settle its part of the suit by paying $55 million, but as part of the settlement did not admit any wrongdoing.[47] Sallie Mae's subsidiary, Southwest Student Services, also settled.

As for Sallie Mae's earlier problems with Cuomo, he let the company off the hook in April 2007, when it voluntarily agreed to change its lending standards to agree with a new Code of Conduct recommended by his office, and to pay $2 million into an educational fund similar to that set up for Nelnet. As *USA Today* reported:

"The nation's largest student loan provider will stop offering perks to college employees as part of a settlement announced Wednesday in a widening probe of the student loan industry.

"SLM Corp., commonly known as Sallie Mae, also agreed to pay $2 million into a fund to educate students and parents about the financial aid industry, and it will adopt a code of conduct created by New York Attorney General Andrew Cuomo, who is heading the probe.

"Cuomo said the expanding investigation of the $85 billion student loan industry has found numerous arrangements that benefitted schools and lenders at the expense of students. Investigators say lenders have provided all-expense-paid trips to exotic locations for college financial aid officers who then directed students to the lenders."[48]

Also in 2007, the U.S. Senate Health, Education, Labor and Pensions (HELP) Committee got a new chairman, Sen. Edward Kennedy, who said it was time "to get the money changers out of the temple, in terms of student loans," and launched several investigations. One focused on misconduct between lenders and universities and another on collection abuses within the industry.[49] The committee sent letters to Nelnet and Sallie Mae. The communication to Nelnet warned the committee had found evidence the company "has refused to provide loan payment and history information to defaulted borrowers and had inappropriately consolidated borrowers' loans without the borrowers' consent."[50]

The letter to Sallie Mae cited the company for:

". Telling a borrower's spouse that the borrower would go to jail if he didn't pay–a blatantly false assertion;

". Putting a borrower into default who lost his home in a natural disaster, adding substantial default and collection fees to his loan balance, taking tax refunds, and garnishing his wages–all in violation of guidelines from the secretary of education;

". Harassing a widower about illegitimate, forged loans under the name of his deceased spouse;
". Refusing to negotiate with borrowers about deferment;
". Regularly calling borrowers at that job after being instructed to stop;
". Harassing borrowers' neighbors, family and coworkers;
". Using abusive and profane language to intimidate borrowers;
". Attempting to collect debts not owed;
". Attempting to collect from deceased borrowers' families and relatives;
". Attempting to collect from elderly, disabled borrowers;
". Firing employees who attempt to help borrowers obtain correct information about their loan status;
". Instructing employees to give borrowers 'the runaround' rather than provide them with correct information on their loan status, and
". Intentionally sending loan payment notices to an incorrect address in order to force a borrower's account into default."[51]

This, and other investigations in the U.S., indicated that high penalties and increased interest levies made it, in Collinge's words, "more profitable for the lenders and guarantors when students defaulted than when they paid"[52] their loans in a normal way, at normal interest levels. And lenders, or the collection agencies who later took over defaulters' accounts, were seemingly willing to go to great lengths to realize those profits. The already-described elimination of legal consumer protections for American student borrowers made it easy.

This is not, of course, to say that such a way of increasing profits was the only motive for all of the abuses investigators discovered. Incompetence, poor training, impatience, and putting the wrong kind of people in charge of a sensitive class of borrowers, probably played a large part, along with short-staffing due to budget cutbacks.

Except for the Edulinx worker quoted earlier in this chapter--to the effect that call centre workers had only six minutes to deal with borrowers–no one has come forward to give an inside view of conditions in either American or Canadian student loan call centres.

However, a worker in a similar British government department recently described conditions there:

"Life in a Department for Work and Pensions call centre.... is like being in a Victorian workhouse. Staff are essentially chained to their desks, monitored for every minute of the day.

"Our priority should be helping people find work and providing a good service to the thousands of vulnerable customers we deal with: pensioners, disabled people, those living in poverty. Instead we have approximately five minutes to deal with each customer; we use outdated systems that are not fit for purpose and essentially we can't do anything to help callers.

"If someone rings for a payment, we are forced to contact an office in another part of the UK and the customer can end up phoning five or six times to get a simple payment issued. At this point a senior manager in the call centre would have to get involved, even though staff who take the calls know how to issue payments. We are not allowed to do this because this will affect our call handling times.

"Jobcentre Plus, part of the DWP, has forcibly transferred 3,500 staff from working on processing benefit claims to handling enquiries by phone in its seven newest call centres. I am one of around 2,400 workers who was on strike yesterday and again today against the oppressive working conditions in these offices.

"It affects every aspect of our jobs. Simple things, such as forms, are not sent out for fear of going over the targets, so we send a message to the already overworked and understaffed processing offices. For many of the people we deal with who are living on the breadline this is simply not good enough.

"We have the skills and experience to help customers but are not permitted to use them; we are purely an answering machine service. The target culture can drive some odd behavior, such as cutting customers off, fobbing them off or even winding them up so they end the call. Some people take shortcuts when dealing with queries; this could result in a massive underpayment or overpayment.

"If we fail to hit the targets or have more than eight days off sick in a year, we are subject to harsh penalties and face the sack. More than 20 per cent of the contact centre workforce has left since April 2010, and this is due to burnout or exhaustion through stress. Mental health-related absences have tripled and morale is at an all-time low.

"We have 19 minutes a day to use for toilet, refreshment and other breaks. Anything over this and you will be classed as 'non-adherent,' which could lead to further penalties."[53]

That, of course, was in the United Kingdom, not the U.S. or Canada, and conditions for North American call centre workers at the time may not have been that bad. Recently, however, signs that budget cutbacks are impacting quality of service in Canadian government call centres–though not specifically those dealing with student loans--were highlighted in a *Globe & Mail* article describing problems with Employment Insurance (EI) centres:[54]

"There is an office within Service Canada where jobless people who have waited undue lengths of time for their first employment-insurance cheque can complain about the delay–

but Service Canada employees are not permitted to tell them about it.

"It's called the Office of Client Satisfaction, and it promises to work to 'resolve any issues brought to its attention.' But call centre agents who field questions about EI claims say they have been warned by their bosses not to mention its existence to the frustrated people on the other end of the line.

" 'The only way they are allowed to give information about it is if the client specifically says 'Do you have information about the Office of Client Satisfaction,' said Steve McCuaig, the national vice-president of the Canada Employment and Immigration Union. 'So how are they supposed to ask for something they don't even know exists?'

"It's a bind that agents find themselves in nmore often as the work force assigned to process claims shrinks to meet federal budget restraints, and the number of EI claims that take more than the maximum 28 days to be decided increases correspondingly."

Plain incompetence or inexperience may also be involved in some student loan mixups. One celebrated tax case in Canada, in which an Ontario small businessman was relentlessly hounded by the Canada Revenue Agency for years, and charged with 28 counts of criminal tax evasion when he had done nothing wrong, and had paid his taxes in full, was recounted on national television.[55] As it turned out, both the auditor and the CRA investigator on the file were beginners, working their very first case. The same could happen with a student loan case.

But, whatever other causes may have been in play, in the U.S., the financial incentive described by Collinge was also there. Theoretically, it was there in Canada as well, at least until the changes in the years after 2000, mentioned previously, but whether it actually did play, or plays a significant role here has not been demonstrated.

At any rate, 2007 was not the best of years for Nelnet Inc., nor had its predecessor been. In 2006, the Canadian government had called for bids on a contract to administer all of its student loans, both those for students in public institutions (up till then administered by Nelnet Canada subsidiary Edulinx/Tricura) and those for students in private schools (at the time, being handled by Resolve). Both Nelnet's Edulinx and Resolve made bids, and in December 2006 Resolve's bid won.

Nelnet spent little time licking its wounds. In May 2007 it sold Edulinx to Resolve.

More than one industry observer was puzzled, not so much by the decision to sell--Edulinx had after all lost a major contract, and Nelnet its erstwhile entree to the Canadian market--but by the decision to award the contract to Resolve. Edulinx, tied as it was to one of the largest U.S. student loan providers and previously in charge of the public institution category of Canadian student loans, seemed to have more than adequate resources to handle the new contract. But Resolve won the bid--and then turned around and acquired those selfsame resources by buying Edulinx.

One critic of the system called it "strange," and compared it to "a drag race," after which the winner promptly bought the loser's engine.

Whatever the reasons for what happened, Resolve had absorbed both Edulinx and Tricura, and now reigned supreme in Canadian student loan servicing.

Roughly a year later, in June 2008, continuing political efforts to reduce the period during which student loans were barred from inclusion in bankruptcy finally bore fruit. The non-dischargeable term was reduced from 10 to seven years. A small but significant victory for Canadian borrowers.

Complaints that the system was too harsh on borrowers, and that repayment terms were often impossible for low-income graduates to comply with, continued to mount, however, and in 2009 the Harper Tories created a mechanism called the Repayment Assistance Plan (RAP), to replace the former Interest Relief and Debt Reduction in Repayment measures. The plan's aim, according to government, was to help "borrowers who are having difficulty paying back their student loan debt." It limited the terms for paying back loans, and made several improvements in the repayment process.

But the RAP soon began encountering the same problems as its predecessors, including difficulties in qualifying for the program, lost electronic applications, telephone staff who seemed not to know the rules, or who appeared to change them at will, contradictory directions, delays in forwarding documents, and many of the other complaints that had been appearing for years on websites like O'Meara's.

Some borrowers began calling it the Repayment Confusion Program.

Regardless of its warts, the new program was at least a gesture towards beleaguered student borrowers. But the right hand giveth, the left hand taketh away. In 2009, the federal government introduced amendments to the Bank Act, specifically exempting student loan borrowers from consumer protection rules that formerly applied to them. Henceforth, lenders would no longer be required to provide student loan borrowers with a statement of the terms of their loan, including interest and discount rates, or with regular statements of the status of payments and balances.

In other words students–alone among Canadians--were to be denied regular reports on how much they owed, how many payments had been credited to their account, or what the interest rates were on their loans.

Canadians were to join their U.S. counterparts, down on the mushroom farm, kept in the dark.

And what of those hapless folk, the defaulters?

After 2009, they no longer had to risk dealing with the kind of screaming, private agency collectors described in Chapter Four, but were in contact with full-time Canada Revenue Agency staff, civil servants. Did this improve matters? Did the removal of even a theoretical profit motive help?

Perhaps and perhaps not.

According to the CRA, it did. Since 2009, "CRA has staff in place to handle telephone enquiries. Each call is handled in a professional manner in addressing the caller's concerns. There are neither quotas nor incentives in place concerning the number of files to be handled by our agents. The CRA is sensitive in its collection approach on Canada Student Loan files. Payment arrangements are established based on an individual's ability to pay."[56]

Evidently, the qualifying phrase "concerning the number of files to be handled" is the key to this statement, since the agency apparently did have a staff incentive system, at least for the five years following May 2006, when a news release announced that Rideau Recognition Solutions Inc. had "signed an initial two-year contract.... to provide rewards and related recognition program services to the employees of the Canada Revenue Agency (CRA)."[57] The contract was renewable for "an additional three years."

According to the release, CRA employees "ensure the economic engine that's supposed to drive Canada." Rideau

CEO Peter Hart added that an incentive system's "economic benefits have been proven in the private sector, in which research shows that improving employee morale by 20 per cent boosts financial performance by 42 per cent. Decades of experience tells [sic] me that public sector agencies that properly employ recognition enjoy similar gains."[58]

Employing Rideau "enhances all of the relationships that impact business performance," he said.

A perusal of Rideau's Website shows the kind of "rewards and related recognition" the company's program advocates.[59] These include "a wide variety of branded products, merchandise gift certificates and travel awards," including such "popular options" as:

"* *Traditional, Emblematic Awards (custom lapel pins, medallions, coins, etc.)*

"* *Heirloom, Heritage and Giftware (watches, clocks, jewellery, writing instruments, crystal art, sculptures, silverware, etc.)*

"* *Lifestyle & Consumer Products (electronics, housewares, sporting goods, optics, tools, books, toys & games, flowers, etc.)*

"* *Corporate Branded Merchandise (apparel, promo items, specialty items, golfing items, etc.)*

"* *Memorabilia & Collectibles (from client-approved and sponsored sources, etc.)*

"* *Travel (packages, experiences, and/or 'a la carte' travel)*

"* *Event Tickets (tickets to various venues, for various events)*

"* *Flowers & Gift Baskets (worldwide)*

"* *Charitable Donations (pending approval of the charity by our clients)*

"* Symbolic, Crafted, Client-Branded Awards (custom plaques, frames, trophies, etc.)
"* Gift Certificates/Gift Cards (retailers gift cards, dependent on region and/or country)
"* Debit Cards (Amex or Visa)
"* Cash Award Management (direct to payroll)."[60]

What, exactly, might constitute the sort of employee activity that helps "boost financial performance" in a government department devoted to collecting taxes or student loan payments, awaits clarification. We do know that it is expected to "impact business performance."

Rideau's Website devotes a page to listing the logos of "our clients." These include, among others, the logo of the Canadian government, and those of six leading banks.

As for the mindset of the employees of Canada Revenue Agency, competing for the rewards offered by such incentive programs, or the workers at HRSDC, where student borrowers' files are handled before they reach the extreme of default, how might it eventually be influenced–for good or ill--by the existence of such award systems, and the pressure to improve "business performance?"

Each employee is an individual, and their value systems may be based on any number of religious, philosophical, or purely practical principles. Their performances may not be overly influenced by merely material rewards. They may not be tempted at all to fudge, to push a borrower a little too hard, or as agents for private collection agencies have been known to do, scream, yell or threaten.

Then there is the case of the HRSDC regional manager, exposed recently for "gross mismanagement." The *Globe & Mail* told her story:

"A middle manager with the federal department of Human Resources who, among other things, used taxpayer dollars to pay for personal massages and was reimbursed for travel that never took place is the first person found guilty of wrongdoing by the Public Sector Integrity Commissioner.

"In a case report Thursday, Mario Dion said the unnamed manager had committed 'gross mismanagement' and misused public funds.

"The actions of the woman, who had been a regional manager of four offices of the HRSDC for more than nine years, were brought to attention by staff in the department's western division. 'They expressed fear for their jobs if they came forward to complain to the department or participated in an investigation,' Mr. Dion says in his report.

"The disclosure stated that many of the staff were frightened of the manager, who they described as an autocrat and a bully who threatened reprisal against employees who questioned the manager. There was fear that in the small communities in which employees resided that retaliation might spread outside the office and affect their family members.'

"The integrity watchdog's investigation determined the manager had misused public funds by approving inappropriate purchases such as personal massages, purchasing equipment such as flat-screen televisions that were not used, paying for lunches for employees, claiming reimbursement for travel that had not occurred, claiming for mileage on her own car when she also had a departmental vehicle, and using government equipment to conduct personal business."[61]

The woman is, of course, not named, and so there is no way to know whether she had anything to do with student loans, or debt repayments. She may have worked in an entirely different section of this large federal department. And her office may not be one of those where the Rideau incentive program is in place. Even if it was, there is no reason to assume it influenced her dishonest behavior. The incentives are, after all, there to reward "financial performance," and good business practice, not dishonesty.

But the student loans system itself, and its culture, have over the years assumed a very different character than that usually associated with the search for knowledge via higher education.

A private loan consultant with a number of student borrower clients[62] had this to say:

"The Canada Student Loans Program is a business. It's no longer an entryway for educational and economic stability for Canadians. It's now a virtual business, a Crown corporate business, and the government's primary concern is keeping people in debt [to keep the business going]. The government just learned how to do business from the banks. They band-aid all kinds of solutions: the Repayment Assistance Program, reducing the 10-year bankruptcy ban to seven years. But it means nothing. The government always does its thing to see that people are indentured. The people that I deal with, that have large student loans, their debts are going to survive their own grown children."

Streamlined ownership

Meanwhile, ownership of the leading federal and provincial *non*-defaulted student loan service providers, simplified when Resolve took over Edulinx/Trucura in 2007, was further streamlined. On 27 July 2009, the Davis + Henderson Income Fund, "through a wholly owned subsidiary acquired all of the outstanding units of Resolve Business Outsourcing Income Fund ("Resolve")."[63] The Davis + Henderson Fund was subsequently converted from "an income trust to a corporate structure," becoming Davis + Henderson Corporation, or D+H, whose business motto is "answers begin with understanding." By streamlined, I mean by corporate-world standards. In actuality the ownership and new lines of authority for Tricura and Resolve, within Davis + Henderson, are a bit complicated, as indicated by the diagram that had to be included in Davis + Henderson's Annual Information Form for 2011.[64]

Davis + Henderson, or its subsidiaries, thus became the kingpin not only of federal student loan administration via the NSLSC, but also of loan administration for those provinces whose student loan regimes are integrated with the Canada Student Loans Program. According to the deputy director of program delivery in the CSLP Directorate, "D+H holds the current contract to administer student financial assistance for the Canada Student Loans Program. Integration agreements are in place with five provinces (ie Ontario, British Columbia, Saskatchewan, New Brunswick and Newfoundland & Labrador), to deliver student financial assistance as a single loan, simplifying the process for the borrower/student. Accordingly, the contract with D+H includes the administration of the provincial portions for the five integrated provinces as well."[65] Davis + Henderson was previously known (and still is) as "the leading provider of cheque supply programs to financial institutions in Canada"–namely the folks who print your cheque books--as well as a manager of "deposit programs (security deposit bags and personalized deposit documents) for financial institutions."[66] Its customers "include the seven largest Canadian financial institutions, credit unions and providers of financial software."[67]

The company also appears now to control, via its Resolve subsidiary, the federal Gun Registry program, and several non-student-loan provincial government programs. For instance, as Resolve Corp., it appears to handle the publications arm of the Ontario government, ServiceOntario Publications.

A finger in many pies.

And who is the individual, human face, or rather who are the faces, of Davis + Henderson?

Since February 2012, its director and chief executive officer has been Gerrard Schmid, who "joined our team as president and CEO of our Filogix Division in July 2009," according to a February 2012 company news release.[68] Before coming to D+H, Schmid had "played important leading roles at Lloyds TSB Bank (United Kingdom) and CIBC's retail bank."[69] He is also a former director of Tricura Canada Inc.[70] His CIBC/Tricura background must stand him in particularly good stead in his new role.

Most of the other members of the D+H board also have banking backgrounds. For example, Michael A. Foulkes is "a former executive of TD Bank Financial Group, having held a variety of executive positions over 30 years with the bank and retiring in late 2006 as president and Chief Executive Officer., TD Waterhouse UK."[71]

William W. Neville was "managing director and head of Citi's North American Hedge Fund Servicing," and "group president, BISYS Banking Solutions Group.[72]

The lone female on the board is Helen K. Sinclair, "founder and Chief Executive Officer of Bankworks Trading Inc.," and a former "president of the Canadian Banking Association."[73]

Gerrard Schmid's name isn't the only one that pops up repeatedly in the history of the various student loan program providers, and the banks connected with the program. An exhaustive list is beyond the scope of this book, but a few names provide a sampling:

Robert Cortina, senior manager web development at Davis + Henderson starting in 2009, had held the same post at Resolve Corporation from 2007 to 2009, and had been technical team leader and then manager of web development at Edulinx Canada Corp. from 2000 to 2007.

Robert C. Ballard, senior vice-president, servicing, for SLM Corporation since February 2012, held several previous posts with Sallie Mae Servicing Corp., and Sallie Mae. He is also listed as former executive vice president and chief operating officer of Alberta Student Loan. He served as executive vice president and chief operating officer of Edulinx Canada Corp. from 1999 to 2001, and as president and chief executive officer of Tricura Canada, as well as chief executive officer of Tricura Technologies Limited.

Gail Kilgour, formerly president and CEO of Edulinx Canada Corporation, senior vice president, government sponsored student loans, Canadian Imperial Bank of Commerce, and senior vice president, e-Business Strategy, CIBC.com, CIBC. Interestingly, she also served for seven years on the board of the University of Guelph, Ontario.

Further down the ladder, Christina Mollo was a Repayment Counselor at Edulinx Canada Corp. From 2002 to 2011, and a supervisor at Tricura from 2002 to 2007.

Such patterns are common enough in most industries. Look at any series of editions of *Editor & Publisher Yearbook*, for example, and many of the same names appear on the mastheads of various newspapers. People know people, move around, and when they move often go where they have ex-co-worker acquaintances, or where previous expertise qualifies them for a similar job.

It's a little like being in a migratory club.

Nor is it unusual to find people with links to banking, like Ms. Kilgour, governing or directing universities, like the University of Guelph. Though Ms. Kilgour seems to have left her post there, the current University of Guelph Board of Governors includes Mary Anne Chambers, retired senior vice president of Scotiabank, and Wendy Millar, executive vice president and chief risk officer, Personal and Commercial Banking, for the BMO Financial Group. She's been with the BMO since 1983.

The president of the University of Alberta, Indira V. Samarasekera, is also a member of the board of directors of the Bank of Nova Scotia.

The University of Victoria Board of Governors includes Ray Protti, previously president and CEO of the Canadian Bankers Association and a co-founder of the International Banking Federation. He was also, notably, a former director of the Canadian Security and Intelligence Service (CSIS).

Nothing unusual in any of this, certainly. Links between banking, political parties, universities, the student loan industry and its current and former service providers are commonplace.

The problem, in Canada, is that this country is a lot smaller than the U.S. and endogamy (marrying within the tribe) in its upper echelons can easily lead to a kind of social "inbreeding." What's good for the "tribe" becomes the rule, whether or not it's good for the rest of us.

Which begs some big, obviously political questions: *ought* banks to be so interwoven with our schools and our government? Should our university campuses, and who gets to study on them, be controlled, directly or indirectly, by banks and a small coterie of bill collectors? Should a steadily increasing percentage of day-to-day government operations, both federal and provincial, be manned not by civil servants subject to government and union regulation, but by employees of a shrinking, consolidating number of private, for-profit corporations, directed by an unelected elite?

Looking at the shambles that has been made of post-secondary educational funding since the Mulroney era, one can't help but wonder if the system as it is today, despite such additions as the Repayment Assistance Program, works at all, and if so, for whom. It doesn't seem to be working well for students or graduates, who should logically be its greatest beneficiaries.

As for its control of what used to be the public civil service, this has been the subject of a warning by the Canadian Centre for Policy Alternatives, a public policy think-tank, that Canadians face the looming prospect of a "shadow" government. According to a Vancouver *Sun* report:[74]

"There's a rapidly expanding shadow public service of private consultants whose ballooning costs will have to be reined in if the government wants to control its spending, a public policy think-tank has warned.

"The growing nature of outsourcing has created a shadow public service that works alongside the real public service but without the same hiring practices or transparency, said the report by the Canadian Centre for Policy Alternatives.

"And it allows public service managers in some cases to skirt bilingualism requirements and other government rules meant to ensure fairness in hiring, it said.

"'Over the past five years, personnel outsourcing costs have risen 79 per cent,' said David Macdonald, researcher within the Ottawa-based think-tank. 'While federal departments have had their budgets capped, expenditures on outside consultants have not been touched and remain above $1 billion a year.

"*'Outsourcing isn't what it used to be,' he said. 'Contractors aren't coming in for a week to do some filing, they are now being hired on contract for years at a time to work beside regular employees.'*"[75]

The report added that, while bid amounts to win outsourcing contracts have been dropping, later cost overruns have caused the actual final cost of such contracts to balloon to "several times the original bid."[76] Four federal departments were named as most notable for outsourcing, one of them being Human Resources and Skills Development Canada (HRSDC), which oversees student loans.

"*While the payrolls of those [four] large departments have increased by less than 10 per cent over the past half decade, their personnel outsourcing costs exploded, rising by 100 per cent, it said.*

"*An extreme example of the shift to a shadow public service cited in the report is at Human Resources, whose outsourcing contracts skyrocketed by 224 per cent over the past decade to $120 million, while its own payroll shrank by four per cent over the same time.*

"*Not only is the outsourcing problem concentrated in four large government departments, it's concentrated among 10 companies, which reap almost 40 cents of every dollar spent on the shadow public service.*"[77]

Third from the top of the 10 companies named was "Resolve Corp., $270.4 million."

Concluded the *Sun* story: "These private companies now receive so much in contracts every year that they have become de-facto wings of government departments, it [the report] said, noting they are insulated from government hiring rules and immune from the Access to Information law."[78]

The article did not mention Rideau Recognition Solutions Inc., with its previous experience in serving banks. According to Rideau's news release announcing its contract with Canada Revenue Agency: "the CRA is the 140th agency or department of the Canadian government to work with Rideau."[79]

1. Stevie Cameron, *On the Take: crime, corruption and greed in the Mulroney years* (Toronto: McClelland-Bantam Inc., 1995), 70.

2. Maude Barlow and Bruce Campbell, *Straight through the heart: how the Liberals abandoned the Just Society* (Toronto: Harper-Collins Publishers Ltd., 1995), 102.

3. Barlow and Campbell, *Op. Cit.*, 57.

4. Parliament of Canada, "*Political contributions by the six largest Canadian banks 1982-2003,*" as posted online at http://www.parl.gc.ca/parlinfo/pages/PartyContributionBank.aspx

5. *Wikipedia, the free encyclopedia*, "Canadian Imperial Bank of Commerce: settlements and controversies," 9, as posted online 15 December 2011 at http://en.wikipedia.org/wiki/Canadian_Imperial_Bank_of_Commerce

6. *Op. Cit.*, 10.

7. *Loc. Cit.*

8. *Loc. Cit.*

9. *Loc. Cit.*

10. *Loc. Cit.*

11. *Loc. Cit.*

12. *Op. Cit.*, 11.

13. Vanessa Lu, "TD Bank ordered to pay $67 million for its role in a $1.2 billion Ponzi scheme," the Toronto *Star*, 19 January 2012, as posted online at http://www.thestar.com/printarticle/1117793

14. Toronto *Star*, *Op.Cit.*

15. *Pocket Criminal Code 2005*, (Toronto: Thomson Canada Limited, 2004, 253-4.

16. *Loc. Cit.*

17. James Scurlock, *Maxed Out: hard times, easy credit and the era of predatory lenders* (New York: Scribner, 2007).

18. Scurlock, *Op. Cit.*, 46.

19. Ross Finnie and Saul Schwartz, *Student Loans in Canada: past, present and future* (Toronto: C.D. Howe Institute, 1996), 85.

20. Finnie and Schwartz, *Op. Cit.*, 83.

21. *Op. Cit.*, 12.

22. *Op. Cit.*, 7.

23. Philippe Brideau, Canada Revenue Agency, private e-mail communication, 23 February 2012.

24. Human Resources and Skills Development Canada, *Canada*

Student Loans Program Annual Report 2007-2008: Part I, 6, as posted online at http://www.hrsdc.gc.ca/eng/learning/canada_student_loan/Publi cations...

25. Sarah Lysecki, "Outsourcer takes over loans from RBC," *it business*, 15 August 2005, as posted online at http://www.itbusiness.ca/it/client/en/Home/News.asp?id=1858.

26. Nelnet Inc., *PR Newswire*, "Nelnet Canada completes acquisition of Edulinx Canada Corporation," 6 December 2004, as posted online at http://www.nelnetinvestors.com/releasedetail.cfm?ReleaseID=1 49867

27. CIBC, Fourth Quarter 2005 News Release, "CIBC announces Fourth Quarter 2005 results," 3.

28. Mark O'Meara, *Canada Student Loans: the need for change*, Coalition for Student Loan Fairness, and CanadaStudentDebt.ca, 1 November 2007.

29. Sue Bailey, "Student loan headaches logged in thousands of cases each month," *The Canadian Press*, 27 April 2004.

30. *Op. Cit.*

31. Peter Boer, "Students chase paper trail," *St. Albert Gazette*, May 2004.

32. O'Meara, *Canada Student Loans*, *Op. Cit.*, 2.

33. April Lindren, "Inspectors focus on XXX video stores,"

National Post, 3 December 2003, as posted online at http://www.wikidfranchise.org/20031203-inspectors-focus

34. Brideau, *Op. Cit.*

35. Alan Michael Collinge, *The Student Loan Scam: the most oppressive debt in U.S. history–and how we can fight back,"* (Boston: Beacon Press, 2009), 44.

36. *Loc. Cit.*, 45.

37. *Wikipedia, the free encyclopedia*, "Nelnet: controversies," 2, as posted online 7 February 2012, at http://en.wikipedia.org/wiki/Nelnet

38. *Wikinvest,* "Nelnet (NNI), " 2, as posted online at ttp://www.wikinvest.com/stock/Nelnet_(NNI)

39. *MSNBC*, "Cuomo: 'It appears that student loan scams don't end at graduation," 3 May 2007, as posted online at http://www.msnbc.msn.com/id/18477803/ns/business-us_business/t/st...

40. *Wikinvest, Op.Cit.*, 2.

41. *Wikipedia*, Nelnet, *Op. Cit.*, 2.

42. *Wikinvest, Op.Cit.*, 2.

43. *Wikipedia, Op. Cit.*

44. *Loc. Cit.*

45. Stephen Burd, "Revisiting the 9.5 per cent student loan scandal," *The Higher Ed Watch Blog*, 23 September 2008, as posted online at http://www.newamerica.net/blog/higher-ed-watch/2008/revisiting-9-5...

46. *Deseret News*, "Student lender Nelnet settles lawsuit for $55 million," 13 August 2010, as posted online at http://www.deseretnews.com/article/print/700056760/Student-lender-...

47. *Deseret News, Op. Cit.*

48. *USA Today*, "Sallie Mae pays $2 million in student-loan scandal settlement," 11 April 2007, as posted online at http://www.usatoday.com/money/industries/banking/2007-04-11-sallie...

49. Collinge, *Op.Cit.*, 49.

50. *Op. Cit.*, 50.

51. *Loc. Cit.*

52. *Op. Cit.*, 14.

53. William Davies, "Working for government call centres makes you sick," the Manchester *Guardian*, 21 January 2011, as posted online at http://www.guardian.co.uk

54. Gloria Galloway, "Service Canada employees told to keep mum on existence of complaints office," 8 November 2011, *The Globe and Mail*, as posted online at http://www.theglobeandmail.com/news/politics/service-canada-

emplo...

55. W5 Staff, "A nightmare when the taxman got it wrong," CTV News, 3 April 2010, as posted online at http://www.ctv.ca/servlet/ArticleNews/print/CTV News/20100401/w5...

56. Brideau, *Op. Cit.*

57. Rideau Recognition Solutions Inc., "Rideau brings recognition to the Canada Revenue Agency," 23 May 2006, as posted online at http://rideau.com/print/news/rideau-brings-recognition-canada-revenu...

58. Rideau, *Op. Cit.*

59. Rideau Inc., "Award Selection," as posted online at http://rideau.com/award-selection

60. *Loc. Cit.*

61. Gloria Galloway, "Integrity czar blasts bureaucrat's bullying, spending habits," 8 March 2012, *The Globe & Mail*, as posted online at http://www.theglobeandmail.com/news/politics/ottawa-notebook/integr...

62. Name withheld at the request of the consultant.

63. *Davis + Henderson*, Davis + Henderson Corporation, Annual Information Form, 14 March 2011, 6.

64. *Op. Cit.*, 8.

65. Private communication, e-mail to Canadian Federation of Students, 26 January 2012.

66. *Davis + Henderson, Op. Cit.*, 9.

67. *Loc. Cit.*

68. D+H, "Davis+Henderson announces appointment of Gerrard Schmid as CEO," 2 February 2012, as posted online at http://dhltd.com/2012/02/davis-henderson-announces-appointment-of-g...

69. *Loc. Cit.*

70. *Land of Free.com*, "Tricura Canada Inc., as posted online at http://canadiancompanies.landoffree.com/company/Tricura_Canada_Inc.

71. D+H, Annual Information, *Op. Cit.*.

72. *Loc. Cit.*

73. *Loc. Cit.*

74. Vancouver *Sun*, "Federal outsourcing has created a 'shadow public service," 4 March 2011, as posted online by Global Services at http://www.globalservicesmedia.com/IT-Outsourcing/Market-Dynamic...

75. *Loc. Cit.*

76. *Loc. Cit.*

77. *Loc. Cit.*

78. *Loc. Cit.*

79. Rideau release, *Op. Cit.*

Chapter Seven: BMOC (Big Money on Campus)

*"But even now worth this,
and now worth nothing?"*

"All that glisters is not gold."

—Shakespeare, *The Merchant of Venice*

At one time, the overall purpose of post-secondary education, not only in Canada but in most of the world, was to develop independent, critical thinkers who were well-grounded in the basic tenets of their civilization and able to integrate the various intellectual disciplines they pursued as specialties–whether chemistry, astronomy, law, medicine or whatever--into a coherent worldview. Or who at least had acquired the tools with which to begin the task.

Learning was to show students not only how to do things, but why they ought to be done.

So crucial was this concern for context that its nature was widely--sometimes sharply--debated, with secularists and partisans of various religions energetically advocating their views.

One of the most famous advocates for a religious context was John Henry Newman, originally an Anglican and later a Roman Catholic clergyman, who was eventually elevated to the lofty post of Cardinal. His 1852 book, *The Idea of a University*,[1] and the preceding series of lectures on which it was based, given in Dublin the same year, constituted a landmark in the history of education in Britain, Ireland and the Western world. So much so, that even those who were not his co-religionists came to share many of his most forceful assertions.

"That only is true enlargement of mind which is the power of viewing many things at once and as a whole, of referring them severally to their true place in the universal system," he wrote.[2]

And then he threw down a blunt gauntlet:

"A thorough knowledge of one science and a superficial acquaintance with many, are not the same thing; a smattering of a hundred things or a memory for detail, is not a philosophical or a comprehensive view. Recreations are not education; accomplishments are not education. Do not say, the people must be educated, when, after all, you only mean amused, refreshed, soothed, put into good spirits and good humor, or kept from vicious excesses. I do not say that such amusements, such occupations of mind, are not a great gain; but they are not education.... [they do] not form or cultivate the intellect. Education is a high word; it is the preparation for knowledge, and it is the imparting of knowledge in proportion to that preparation..........

"A university is an Alma Mater, knowing her children one by one, not a foundry, or a mint, or a treadmill."[3]

If Newman could see the average Canadian campus, after decades of cutbacks in government funding, years of burgeoning tuition fees, the confused and vicious workings of the student loan system, and the general drift toward privatization, he would probably be rolling in his grave.

Stockholm Syndrome

The cutbacks described in Chapter Six, in both federal transfer payments for education and provincial education budgets, forced universities into an ever-more-frantic scramble for the cash needed to operate. They became hostages to the dollar and, like many hostages, some eventually exhibited a kind of Stockholm Syndrome, adopting a profit-oriented view more radical than the miserly governments whose parsimony had made them prisoners in the first place.

Colleges and universities have come increasingly to see themselves as businesses selling a product, commonly defined as specialist knowledge of a given discipline. When the transfer of that knowledge is complete, it is stamped with a credential that serves as a *de facto* warranty: the diploma or degree. Students are consumers of that product, paying customers and no more.

The requirements of the modern job market make students captive consumers–they need the product to get a job and survive–and the loan system makes them effectively captives-at-any-price. They too are hostage.

As for research expertise, the other half of the university's traditional task, it has also become a product, stamped with a warranty in the form of a patent or publication, which can be rented or sold to the corporate sector. In this case the paying consumer/corporate donor is not so much hostage as hostage-taker, supplying research grants and funds, and defining the goals and parameters of the research paid for.

And how does a campus full of dollar hostages and hostage-takers act?

It acts like any Big Box discount store, whose basic priorities are to reduce overhead and cut costs, while boosting sales volume. The Miser Marts of the world all seem to run on skeleton staffs. Trying to find a sales person, or "associate," when you need one means wandering up and down the aisles, traversing half the store. And when one is found, he or she often knows nothing about the tools or clothes or clocks or toys you want to buy. Underpaid and probably overworked, such folk are counting the minutes to closing time, when they can go home.

In the halls of academe, the story is much the same. At good old Miserly U., teacher-to-student class ratios are the equivalent of retail sales staff-to-customer ratios. In first year, especially, lecture amphitheaters with upwards of 100-200 spectator seats are common, with a single professor down in the pit, shouting to be heard in the bleachers. According to the Toronto *Globe & Mail*, some university lecture halls seat 500 students.[4] If this is true, how any lecturer, even with help from one or two graduate teaching assistants, could hope to give individual attention to 500 first-year students per semester is beyond imagination.

But, as TV's David Letterman likes to say, it's "volume, volume, volume" in the discount business.

For decades, across Canada, "schools have boosted enrolment faster than they hired new faculty."[5] As *Education This Week* reported: "From 1994 to 2007 full-time [student] enrolment in Canada increased by about 40 per cent, the number of full-time faculty increased by an estimated 12 per cent, and the student to faculty ratio increased by almost one-quarter," while "Ontario's student to faculty ratio was almost 40 per cent worse than public universities in the United States."[6]

Statistically, the ratio of full-time students to full-time faculty in Ontario rose from 17-1 to 25-1 between 1988 and 2008[7] (not all courses are of the amphitheater type).

A jump of eight students per teacher per course may not seem like much to the layperson, but multiply by eight the number of hours spent developing, administering and correcting an average of two to five, 20-50-page term papers or projects, 5-10 class quizzes, a midterm and final examination, and after-class counseling of students in the teacher's office, per course, per semester and it is no small thing.

This author taught as a full-time professor at one American and two Canadian universities, with a usual class load of three, more rarely four courses per semester. Adding eight students per class, per semester–24 students--would have meant a *minimum* increase of 48 term papers, 120 quizzes, 24 midterm and 24 final exams, and God alone knows how many more hours per week spent counseling students one-on-one in my office.

It could be done, in fact is done. Several of my courses had 30 students. But there were no weekends free, and no evenings either. One routinely worked 12-hour days, seven days a week, taking breaks only at risk of falling behind.

Only in semesters when I was doing approved research, and hence was allowed a lighter course load, was there time to breathe.

And the average cited above, of 25-1, is only for Ontario, and an average. Some individual schools are far worse. At the University of Ontario Institute of Technology, for instance, the full-time teacher-to-student ratio stood at 53-1 in a 2010 survey.[8]

Of course, full-time, tenured or tenure-track professors still enjoy reasonably good pay and pension schemes. Not only do they work hard, but they are–or ought to be--the top people in their fields, with national or international reputations and years of professional accomplishment. They often have in-depth industry experience, have won numerous awards, and have lists of published books and scholarly articles after their names.

Those in the sciences and engineering may hold multiple patents, and be advisors to foundations or to government. Maintaining the pay and pension packages needed to retain such folk, on whose presence a university's reputation may depend, becomes harder and harder in an era when government support is melting like the polar caps in a time of global warming. The fastest-growing operating cost at many universities is often the pension fund, and, as recent press reports indicate, too many funds are in the hole.

According to a *Globe & Mail* article: "The University of Guelph faces a [pension] shortfall of $344 million. York University's is $339 million. The University of Ottawa's is $206 million. McMaster's is $301 million. One of the worst problems is at Dalhousie, where the pension shortfall has doubled in a year to a whopping $270 million. That works out to almost $100,000 per plan member."[9]

With such numbers against them, and senior faculty unable or unwilling to take on yet-more-impossible workloads, the obvious solution is to put the burden on students, and on part-time faculty.

And thereby hangs a tale, or more accurately a vexed question all its own.

As the *New York Times* has pointed out:

"If you've written a few five-figure tuition cheques or taken on 10 years of debt, you probably think you're paying to be taught by full-time professors. But it's entirely possible that most of your teachers are freelancers.

"In 1960, 75 per cent of college instructors were full-time tenured or tenure-track professors; today only 27 per cent are. The rest are graduate students or adjunct and contingent faculty–instructors employed on a per-course or yearly contract basis, usually without benefits and earning a third or less of what their tenured colleagues make....

"It's sometimes harder to track down adjuncts outside of class, because they rarely have offices or even their own departmental mailboxes.

"Many patch together jobs at different colleges to make ends meet, and with commuting, there's less time to confer with students or prepare for class. It's not unusual for adjuncts to be hired at the last minute to teach courses they've never taught. And with no job security, they may consider it advantageous to tailor classes for student approval."[10]

What are the differences between full-time and part-time instructors? A U.S. geology professor explained:

"Full-time faculty do a lot more than teach. They serve as department chairs and program coordinators. They do periodic program and course evaluations required, in our case, by the State University of New York system in Albany. They develop new programs and courses. They serve on various committees which determine academic policy, hear student grievances, and plan the future direction of the college. They advise and register students each semester. They do research. They engage in professional development. They give talks and lectures outside their classes. Just a few examples....

"Adjunct faculty generally do none of these things. They typically come in, teach their course, and maybe hold one office hour a week."[11]

The *Times*, and the geology professor, were speaking about U.S. schools, but the picture is not much different in Canada-- and no wonder when one considers how Canadian sessionals are treated. Take one sessional interviewed by the Ottawa *Citizen*, for example:

"*Last winter, Irene Smolnik worked 12-hour to 16-hour days, seven days a week, for four months, to earn a grand total of $15,000.*

"*Broken down into an hourly wage, that's not much more than a grocery store clerk makes. Ms. Smolnik, however, has a PhD in sociology and is a sessional lecturer at Carleton University and the University of Ottawa.*

"*The three courses she taught last winter required extensive preparation, since she'd never taught them before, but she was paid only for her time in the classroom and not for the hours she spent mastering the new material....*

"*Ms. Smolnik has no benefits, no job security and no time to do the work that might get her a shot at a tenure-track job: research and writing.*"[12]

Not surprisingly, part time instructors on both sides of the border are unhappy with their lot. A survey of part-time instructors published by the American Federation of Teachers showed that "about 57 per cent say their salaries are falling short," and "41 per cent of those surveyed say that their job security is falling short of expectations."[13] It added that "the working conditions and job security of America's part-time/adjunct faculty leave a great deal to be desired."

The lack of opportunity for research, cited by Ms. Smolnik in the *Citizen*, is a crucial factor. To be truly on top of a given specialist discipline, a teacher should be aware of the latest developments in it, and preferably contributing to those developments, helping push forward its frontiers with projects of his or her own. A good professor ought to subscribe to and regularly read the leading journals in that specialty and in specialties related to it, should be in contact with other leading specialists in his or her field, and should attend the most important meetings and conferences devoted to new developments.

Sessionals can't do this. They haven't the time, nor the research budgets, nor the travel budgets for it. They're lucky to be able to make their monthly mortgage payments, and the daily commute. Even if they did find time to write a professional paper, what scholarly journal would take a submission seriously, coming from an unknown, part-time staffer with no standing and no one to vouch for their work?

With the best will in the world, the cards are stacked against them. Sessionals, by the nature of their positions, have second-class status, and their students are, at least by inference, getting second-class instruction. This is not to say that individual sessionals are not good teachers, or well-qualified in their fields. But as a general rule, they must operate, and teach at a disadvantage.

A university that entrusts more than 70 per cent of its undergraduate classroom instruction to part-time staff is short-changing its students. It is also hampering its research potential, by denying talented part-time staff, who might be able to contribute to the advancement of knowledge, the support and time needed to do so.

And what of the overall nature and quality of Miserly U.'s research efforts, quite apart from the subject of sessional staff?

Crabbed, narrow and hidden

First, it is chronically under-funded from the government side, a point that the Canadian Association of University Teachers (CAUT) keeps making. And inevitably, as private corporate funding takes the place of public money, by its nature, Miserly U.'s research must become more and more crabbed, narrow and--perhaps worst of all--hidden.

The provinces have been cutting research funding for years. Most recently, Ontario's Liberal government scrapped $42 million in university research grants, only days before launching a much-vaunted tuition rebate for undergraduates.[14]

At the federal level, as the CAUT noted in a 2007 submission to the House Standing Committee on Finance prior to the 2008 budget, funding cuts to post secondary education had been going on for decades, and "in 1996, with the introduction of the Canada Health and Social Transfer (CHST), cash transfers to the provinces for post-secondary education, health and social assistance were reduced by nearly $7 billion."[15] The increases earmarked for the 2008-9 budget, the submission said, "fall more than $1.2 billion short of what would be needed just to restore funding to 1992-93 levels, adjusting for inflation and population growth."[16]

Barely more than a budget cycle later, the CAUT was writing Tory Finance Minister Jim Flaherty on the same topic, with similar arguments, lamenting that "Last year..... funding for the conduct of research through Canada's three granting agencies was actually reduced by $147 million.....[17] Cuts to the granting agencies and the uncertainty about continued federal support for a number of research foundations and bodies have cast a cloud over the future of university-based science."

The CAUT was not only concerned about the overall lack of funding for research, but "deeply troubled by how your government is increasingly actively directing what research is done. The 2009 budget allocated $87.5 million for new Canada Graduate Scholarships but specified that 'scholarships granted by the Social Sciences and Humanities Research Council will be focused on business-related degrees.' The budget also stipulated that the bulk of infrastructure money given to the

Canadian Foundation for Innovation is for future priority projects identified by the Minister of Industry."[18]

"This is not a new problem, but it is one that seems to be growing more common with each passing budget..... History has shown us that decisions about the merits of scientific research are best left to scientists, not governments or politicians. The world's most important and innovative scientific discoveries have typically come from basic research, driven by researchers' quest for knowledge, with a scientific peer-review process making decisions about what areas and what research to fund."[19]

Here, the CAUT had put its finger on a real threat, identifying a major danger of the myopic, business-profit-is-everything approach. It is a danger with several facets:

1) There is an inherent injustice in using the facilities and staff of public universities, supported at least in part by everyone's tax dollars, to conduct research that will be used to increase the profits of private business;
2) An obvious imbalance is created if a rising percentage of public money is devoted to supporting only those projects–or even those faculties--which directly benefit business, or those that have an immediate business application, while starving other research of support;
3) Cutting back government funds and forcing universities to rely on private, corporate funding narrows research choices still further;
4) Privately supported, corporate-funded research tends to be proprietary, namely its results are owned by the donor that supported it, and only that donor.

Corporate donors, if they are footing the bill for a professor's or a department's research, not only want to set the parameters of a project, to assure its results will be directly translatable to commercial use, but also to keep those results hidden from their business competitors.

Thus the traditional working method of science, accepted as basic for centuries, is short-circuited.

In the past, researchers were anxious to boast of and share their finds, publishing them widely in journals, thereby making the information available to others working in the same area. One scholar's discovery, shared with peers, could thus spark others' research, one advance building upon another. As the saying went, every innovator "stood on the shoulders" of those who went before.

Now, corporate-funded researchers may be encouraged, even obliged by contract terms, to do the opposite. Their research is not-to-be-shared with others, who once might have built on their work to further advance a discipline.

Paradoxically, the speed of scientific advance, in some areas, can slow to a crawl, precisely because researchers are no longer cooperators, but competitors. As individual sprinters, rather than relay teams, they may be in a race, and hurrying, but the overall scientific track is running in reverse. The racers are running up the down staircase.

And some find they aren't in the race at all.

Scholars who want to do so-called "pure research," namely "curiosity-driven" investigations into aspects of a subject others may not have considered, are increasingly hampered by the dominant attitude that to be worth anyone's time and money, research goals must be strictly practical and short-term. Under such a regime, most of the 20th century's advances in theoretical physics, or astronomy, or environmental biology would never have happened.

The National Graduate Caucus of the Canadian Federation of Students issued a stark warning about this in 2009, in a paper titled *Public Risk, Private Gain*.[20] Recalling the history of the three federal granting organizations--the Canadian Institutes of Health Research (CIHR), the Natural Sciences and Engineering Research Council (NSERC), and the Social Sciences and Humanities Research Council (SSHRC)--it pointed out that:

"The granting councils were originally established to foster curiosity-driven research through the expansion of funding opportunities to faculty and graduate students. Yet the federal government's rush to commercialize university research is increasingly at odds with the councils' peer-reviewed and independent research projects."[21]

The new policy of measuring everything by its potential dollar value has serious drawbacks, including:

* Disproportionate support: "Even though over 60 per cent of students study in the Social Sciences and Humanities, SSHRC receives significantly less funding than other granting councils;"[22]

(This complaint echoed an earlier one by the CAUT, deploring "the federal government's initiative to reorient the focus of our entire university system away from the social sciences and humanities. Whereas more than half of all students choose to study in the social sciences and humanities and more than half of all faculty teach in these areas, 80 per cent of Canada Research Chairs are designated to be in the natural and health sciences.")[23]

* Tunnel vision: "Funding increasingly supports disciplines that are considered 'natural' allies of business;"[24]

* Anti-arts bias: "Graduate students studying in the liberal arts are often competing for limited funds to study, while

students in applied disciplines may be able to survive on comfortable stipends throughout their programs;"[25]

Evidence of such bias was provided by the recent decision of Ontario's Queen's University to suspend enrolment in its Fine Arts program, despite high student demand for its courses. Reported the *Globe & Mail*:

"Queen's University is suspending enrolment to its Bachelor of Fine Arts program, citing a shortage of necessary resources to sustain it.... The decision to halt new enrolments for 2012-13 is not a sign of declining interest in the program, however, said Kathleen Sellars, an associate professor and the BFA program director. Ms. Sellars confirmed that 30 new first-year students enrolled this fall–the program's capacity–and that 107 students are taking the program overall."[26]

* Market haggling: "University researchers are increasingly bogged down in a new role seeking investors, negotiating contracts, and haggling over publishing rights. All of this effort detracts from laboratory and teaching time–what Canadians have traditionally expected from university professors;"[27]

* Secrecy: "Innovation is stalled in the wider scholarly community when research results are kept secret.... Industry is oriented towards secrecy to gain a competitive advantage, while academe requires open dialogue and debate for peer assessment;"[28]

Added the report:

"In one study, 1,077 graduate students and post-doctoral students were surveyed in the life sciences, computer science and chemical engineering. Approximately one-quarter reported that they had been denied information relevant to their research at some point. This was especially prevalent in research groups with links to industry. About half the affected respondents reported delays to their research."[29]

Far more disturbing, not only in terms of academic honesty but of public safety, was the situation "when the university-industry partnership involves public health" and pollution standards were at stake. "The corporate infiltration of a panel convened to set standards for chromium (VI) in California succeeded in skewing the panel's decision to protect industry profits rather than public health."[30]

Suppression or omission of data or falsification of research results to favor a particular economic or political bias is becoming more common, while exposing such dishonesty is growing more dangerous. Warned the report:

"Governments are aggressively pushing the commercialization agenda but are negligent in providing adequate protections for researchers who come forward to highlight threats to research integrity. Commonly known as whistleblowers, researchers who report data suppression or more blatant misconduct have no formal protection. Coming forward in the name of the public interest can be a career-ending decision."[31]

Whistleblowers who expose dishonest research are not the only ones facing opprobrium, according to an article in the Toronto *Star* in 2011.[32] The story cited the cases of four academics who claimed they were targeted by the Conservative government for their research findings, including political scientist Peter Langille:

"Langille, an outspoken professor with a PhD in peace studies, had problems with Canada's defense establishment long before Western [University of Western Ontario] hired him in 1997. In 2005, he was the lone academic to testify before a parliamentary committee about soaring cost overruns and equipment problems with four Upholder-class submarines the Canadian Forces purchased from the Royal Navy. Moreover, he

told the committee that military and strategic studies programs at universities are 'deliberately structured to establish a supportive academic constituency.'

"At Western, he says he ran afoul of a mindset in senior levels of the political science department that cringed over his criticism of government-supported defense programs and, ultimately, the Harper team over its failure to send Canadian peacekeepers to genocide-ravaged Darfur.

"His final course was dropped from the curriculum even as he completed a prestigious post-doctorate fellowship in 2006-07 and served as a poster boy for Western as a featured speaker at global conferences."[33]

And then there is the case of the closing of Canada's northernmost research station, the Polar Environment Atmospheric Research Laboratory (PEARL), whose demise could be laid to any one of several factors, from political bias to the fact that no commercial business was making a direct profit from its findings. Located on Ellesmere Island, the lab's annual $1.5 million funding was cut off as of 30 April 2012.

"We've hit the wall," said James Drummond, an atmospheric physicist at Dalhousie University in Nova Scotia, who worked there, adding that the station had been an important centre for high-latitude, high-altitude research and has helped shed light on issues from climate change to the Arctic ozone hole.[34] Added a *Canadian Press* (CP) story:

"Drummond said [competitions for funding] are increasingly stacked against basic research programs.

"'We never managed to fit the very narrow criteria that funding is being allocated on now,' he said. 'Often (the parameters are) that industry will benefit.'

"While academic committees award the grants, the criteria used are influenced by government policy, said Drummond.

'This move toward much more applied, industry-focused granting is a political dimension.... Generally, it's very difficult to do something that is high-budget and at a research level that is of benefit to the globe rather than to a small section of the population like a company,' he said.'"[35]

The fact that the station's work dealt with the highly-politicized question of global warming may also have told against it. Noted the CP story: "Drummond said PEARL has played an important part in several significant breakthroughs. The fact PEARL operated through the polar winter made it unique and allowed it to prove that's when climate change in the Arctic is most severe."[36]

Risky investment
Finally, to the list of dangers connected with the commercialization of our campuses, add the pitfalls of investment.

Depending as they increasingly must on their own income sources, universities may turn to investment to save themselves. And sometimes those investments can bring problems hitherto unknown to the Halls of Academe. Such was the situation recently when the Oakland Institute charged that prominent American universities, including Harvard and Vanderbilt Universities and Spelman College, were investing in hedge funds and companies that are driving African farmers off their land. According to a news report:

"The California-based think-tank, which focuses on social, economic and environmental issues..... alleges that these investments are increasing price volatility and supply insecurity in the global food chain, and not returning to African nations the benefits that were promised.

"The main link the reports establish between Harvard, Vanderbilt and Spelman and land development in Africa is a London-based hedge fund called Emergent Asset Management.... that purchases and develops agricultural land to produce products for export.... The report states that other universities might be making similar investments with different companies.....

"The report argues that.... 'these largely unregulated land purchases are resulting in virtually none of the promised benefits for native populations, but instead are forcing millions of small farmers off ancestral lands and small, local food farms in order to make room for export commodities, including biofuels and cut flowers.'"[37]

The story took care to note that the company in question insisted it was doing good, and even if it wasn't that the universities might be "unaware" of the implications of their investment. "Given the pressure on endowment managers to produce healthy returns," it added, there is bound to be "risk."

Of course there is. And it will keep right on growing. One can almost hear Gordon Gekko calling, in the soothing tones of a tempter: "Greed is good, greed is good....... "

Privatization, commercialization and debt are all slices of the same pie.

1. This book has been published in many editions. That quoted here is: John Henry Cardinal Newman, *The Idea of a University* (Notre Dame, Indiana: University of Notre Dame Press, 1982).

2. Newman, *Op. Cit.*, 103.

3. *Op. Cit.*, 109.

4. Globe Editorial, "Canadian universities must reform or perish," *The Globe & Mail*, 10 October 2011, as posted online at http://www.theglobeandmail.com/news/opinions/editorials/canadian-u...

5. James Bradshaw, "For undergrads at Canada's universities, a new way of learning," *The Globe & Mail*, 15 September 2011, as posted online at http://www.theglobeandmail.com/news/national/education/universityn...

6. Ken Snowdon, "The quality challenge: the case for more faculty," *Education This Week* (Canadian Edition), 30 April 2010, as posted online at http://www.educationalpolicy.org/publications/etw/canada/commentary...

7. Globe Editorial, *Op. Cit.*

8. University of Ontario Institute of Technology Faculty Association, "UOIT has the highest student-faculty ratio in Canada!! 53:1," *A the Table*, 15 April 2010, 1.

9. Margaret Wente, "Pension ponzi is a raw deal for students,"

The Globe & Mail, 6 December 2011, as posted online at http://www.theglobeandmail.com/news/opinions/margaret-wente/pensi...

10. Samantha Stainburn, "The case of the vanishing full-time professor," the New York *Times*, 3 January 2010, as posted online at http://www.nytimes.com/2010/01/03/education/edlife/03strategy-t.htm...

11. Steven Schimmrich, "Full-time vs. adjunct faculty," *Hudson Valley Geologist*, 10 January 2010, as posted online at http://hudsonvalleygeologist.blogspot.com/2010/01/full-time-vs-adnunc...

12. No byline, "The unappreciated plight of the underpaid 'roads' scholar," The Ottawa *Citizen*, 7 November 2005, as posted online at http://www.canada.com/story_print.html?id=22cb8172-a706-498e-9f4...

13. American Federation of Teachers, "A national survey of part-time/adjunct faculty," *American Academic*, Vol. 2, March 2010, 3.

14. Tanya Talaga, "University research grants scrapped by Liberals," The Toronto *Star*, 6 January 2012, as posted online at http://www.thestar.com/printarticle/1111885.

15. Canadian Association of University Teachers, "Statement to the House of Commons Standing Committee on Finance regarding the 2007 Pre-Budget Consultations," August 2007, as

posted online at http://www.caut.ca/pages.asp?page=584

16. *Loc. Cit.*

17. Penny Stewart, president and James L. Turk, executive director, Canadian Association of University Teachers, letter to Hon. Jim Flaherty, House of Commons, 16 February 2010, 1.

18. Stewart and Turk, *Op.Cit.*, 2.

19. *Loc. Cit.*

20. National Graduate Caucus, Canadian Federation of Students, "Public Risk, Private Gain: an introduction to the commercialization of university research," 2009.

21. Caucus, *Op. Cit.*, 3.

22. *Loc. Cit.*

23. James L. Turk, executive director, Canadian Association of University Teachers, "Canadian post-secondary education at a crossroads," 27 November 2005, presentation to the National Dialogue on Higher Education, Ottawa, as posted online at http://www.caut.ca/pages.asp?page=452.

24. *Loc. Cit.*

25. *Op. Cit.*, 4.

26. James Bradshaw, "Queen's University suspends its fine arts program, citing shortage of resources," *The Globe & Mail*, 10 November 2011, as posted online at

http://www.theglobeandmail.com/news/national/queens-university-sus....

27. *Op. Cit.*, 5.

28. *Loc. Cit.*

29. *Loc. Cit.*

30. *Op. Cit.*, 6.

31. *Op. Cit.*, 7.

32. Linda Diebel, "Defence industry critic claims he was blacklisted over political views," 16 March 2011, The Toronto *Star*, as posted online at http://www.thestar.com/printarticle/954605.

33. Diebel, *Op. Cit.*

34. Bob Weber, "PEARL beyond price: Arctic scientists give up on research station funding," *The Canadian Press*, 28 February 2012, as posted online at http://www.printthis.clickability.com/pt/cpt?expire=&title=PEARL+b...

35. Weber, *Op. Cit.*

36. *Loc. Cit.*

37. Kevin Kiley, "Open land, closed books," 21 June 2011, Inside Higher Ed, *Truthout*, as posted online at http://www.truth-out.org/open-lands-closed-books/1308667796

Chapter Eight: "The population wants it."

*"A substitute shines brightly as a king,
until a king be by."*

*"It is twice blessed:
it blesseth him that gives, and him that takes."*

--Shakespeare, *The Merchant of Venice*

There was an old Vaudeville routine, called "The Batter." The scene would open onstage with a man standing there in the spotlight, laughing and cackling maniacally, and hitting himself on the head with a baseball bat. Of course, the bat was made of foam rubber or cardboard, so as not to injure the comedian. An Interlocutor would come onstage, and stand looking at the Maniac.
Interlocutor - Why are you hitting yourself on the head with a baseball bat?
Maniac (laughing and cackling) - Because it feels so good when I stop!
Interlocutor (after a pause and double-take) - Then why don't you stop, and feel good?
Maniac - Because I want to feel EVEN BETTER!!!
There are a couple of other bats lying on the ground next to the Maniac. The Interlocutor picks up a bat, and starts hitting himself on the head. The two start whacking their heads in sync, laughing and shouting:
Maniac and Interlocutor - Better and better!!!!!!!!

It was the perfect illustration of Chesterton's "logic of the madhouse."

If one stands back and looks at the current system of financing post-secondary education in Canada, one gets the uncanny feeling that it is really some sort of Vaudeville act. In fact, the entire national economy seems based on a kind of twisted logic, that we, as Interlocutor-straight men, appear to have accepted.

If it had background music, it would be the tune of Granada, with the lyric: "Austerity, I'm falling under your spell........"

Whack, whack. Better and better.

Where to look, and where not

Anyone with the patience to have read through the preceding chapters likely understands that our current way of paying for higher education is a disaster. It's time we put a stop to Canada's student loan pain. The question is how best to do it.

There are a number of paths to a solution, but one direction *not* to take is that of "more of the same," to keep on hitting ourselves on the head with a bat.

The latter actually is the solution offered by such folks as Bob Rae, by the federal Liberals' Canadian Millennium Scholarship Foundation (MSF), by various spokespersons for the right-tending Education Policy Institute (EPI), and by both the Harper Tories in Ottawa and the McGuinty Liberals in Ontario. All insist that universities and colleges ought to keep on raising tuition–the sky is the limit--while students should keep on dealing with it by volunteering for greater--and still greater--debt.

Some of the arguments advanced to support the status quo border on the ridiculous. For example, that expressed by Rae following his 2005 report for the Ontario government, "Ontario: a leader in learning,"[1] and by the authors of various MSF[2] and EPI publications and statements, that *not* raising tuition amounts to a "subsidy for the rich."

Here, one is tempted, like the Interlocutor, to do a double-take, and perhaps imagine this applied to other retail products, like groceries. If *filet mignon* and Russian caviar are so high-priced that only the rich can afford them, to reduce their price– so that everyone, or at least middle-class shoppers–could afford them is, well, pampering the rich. Of course, the rich can already afford them, just as they can already easily afford a university education, but making it possible for others to do so-- is making it too easy for the rich. Instead of price being a mere afterthought, this would allow them not to have to think about it at all. Better to let the rest of us go without.

Only where education is concerned we're not talking about caviar-style luxuries, but about basics. It's closer to pricing bread itself out of the reach of everyone, then refusing to reduce the price on grounds it would subsidize the rich. Better to let the rest of us starve. Or not go to school.

Such nonsense shouldn't have much traction, but it is typically dressed up in graphs and columns of statistics, as in "lies, damned lies and statistics," and governments that receive a great deal of election support from the banking sector appear to find them captivating. Anyone else who may be so tempted need only read economist Hugh Mackenzie's rebuttal to Rae, *The Tuition Trap*,[3] for a detailed and thorough demonstration, giving due attention to those graphs and statistics, of how false the argument is.

Going into it further here would be a waste of space.

Not all advocates of the "more of the same" approach lean on such sophistry, however. Some, like former TD Bank Chief

Economist Don Drummond, appointed to head an Ontario Public Service Reform Commission, insist that an overarching need for "fiscal austerity" dictates not only raising post-secondary tuition, but even dipping down into elementary and secondary school levels to impose new, or higher fees there as well. For instance ex-banker Drummond, in a report that Ontario Premier Dalton McGuinty praised as "objective and clinical,"[4] advocates raising class sizes in elementary school, cancelling cuts in college and university tuition, and imposing user fees on children who travel to their classes on school buses.[5]

The need for austerity, trumpeted these days by banks and government finance ministers, is presented as the only solution to a supposed "fiscal crisis" in government budgets. Governments are running frightening deficits, the argument goes, and so we must "tighten our belts," and eliminate, or at least cut back, various public services, particularly health care and public education.

What the bankers and finance ministers don't mention is what caused those budget shortfalls in the first place. Worldwide, the biggest deficits have been caused by a) the bursting of various credit bubbles created by the banks themselves, and the resultant demand for massive government-funded "bailouts," and, b) tax cuts brought in by governments, particularly cuts in corporate taxes–including those for banks. The U.S. involvement in its multiple, staggeringly expensive wars has added to its own particular money-crunch.

In Canada, due to better regulation of the domestic banking industry, we've escaped the worst of the credit bubbles, but not the tax cuts. The year following the Harper government's first election victory in 2006, Tory Finance Minister Jim Flaherty introduced a five-year, $60 billion tax cut. That cut had been preceded by former Liberal Finance Minister Paul Martin's $100 billion income tax cut over five years, starting in 2000. In addition, $12 billion was being lost each year by lowering the Goods and Services Tax from seven to five per cent.

Federal corporate tax cuts were scheduled to rise even more steeply by 2012-13, to $14.8 billion, with the corporate tax rate falling to 15 per cent–the lowest in the G7 nations.

As columnist Murray Dobbin wrote:

"Without all those tax cuts, it is arguable that there would be no deficit at all. Not only that, of course, we could have been spending that money on the collective needs of Canadians–municipal infrastructure, national child care, pharmacare, lowered tuition fees, money for greening the economy. Target industrial development."[6]

As a U.S. commentator on Canadian affairs put it: "By creating the deficit, Harper has created the crisis."[7]

At provincial level, the story was much the same. As the Ontario Public Service Employees Union (OPSEU) commented, the various tax cuts made over the years by the Mike Harris Tories and then by the McGuinty Liberals totaled roughly "$16 billion less in revenue for the Ontario government every year. $16 billion–hey, isn't that what Drummond and [Ontario Finance Minister Dwight] Duncan say is the present deficit?"[8]

Added the union's commentary:

"Economic growth comes from two sources–the private sector and the public sector. For every dollar the public sector spends, it usually creates a ripple effect in the economy of about $1.50. If the public sector sheds jobs too quickly, the private sector has to make up for it or run the risk of recession. This is called fiscal drag. If Drummond's recommendations to limit spending are accepted, according to economist Jim Stafford, this could reduce economic growth from between 1.6 per cent to

2.8 per cent over the next four years. That's a huge obstacle for the private sector to overcome. "If we go into recession, government revenues fall farther, creating the need for another cycle of cuts."[9]

Writing from a European viewpoint, on the Standard & Poor agency's threat to downgrade Eurozone countries' credit ratings, a Manchester *Guardian* contributor noted:
"Where to find the resources for these massive bailouts of the private banking system? The orthodox, 'monaterist' and economically deeply flawed answer is 'savings.' These, it is argued, can only be found by way of 'austerity.' That is, for example, by gutting government investment in the economy, impoverishing pensioners and making millions of Europeans unemployed.

"But as S&P can see as clearly as any little boy in the crowd, 'austerity' has no economic clothes. Austerity is destroying investment and jobs, and therefore income. Without employment, individuals, households, firms and governments are deprived of money. Without employment income, governments cannot collect taxes, and banks cannot collect debt repayments. So banks face bankruptcy and government deficits rise. It's not complicated."[10]

In short, it's a self-made, self-perpetuating crisis. Something like hitting ourselves on the head with a baseball bat. The sheer, crazy short-sightedness of it should be amazing, but if you stand up in public and say something with a straight enough face........

Million dollar degree

Another argument advanced by proponents of ever-higher tuition is that a university degree is worth so much--in terms of the extra lifetime earnings of its holder, compared to those of high school graduates--that students should be willing to pay almost anything for it. The usual figure cited is "the Million Dollar Degree."

The term is catchy, and so has been repeated over and over. It has also been debated over and over, from a variety of angles, and generally shown to be both over-simplified and exaggerated. Mackenzie devotes a significant part of his tuition study to graduate earnings, and describes the pitfalls of oversimplifications like the $1 million degree.[11]

University graduates do tend, on average, to make more than those with less education, but the $1 million figure is hard to justify. Various critics have pegged the true premium at between $200,000 and $300,000, for certain graduates under certain circumstances, over their lifetimes. American education critic Charles Miller, who headed U.S. Secretary of Education Margaret Spelling's Commission on the Future of Higher Education, claims $279,893. The Organization for Economic Cooperation and Development (OECD) puts the figure even lower, at roughly US$ 145,000 in the 31 OECD countries.[12]

But not for everyone. Having a bachelor's degree is far from a guarantee of riches, or even of having a good job. As the *Globe & Mail* reported:

""On average, Canadian university graduates do well over a career.... But nearly one in five–more than any other country in the Organization for Economic Cooperation and Development (OECD)–still wind up at the low end of the economic scale..... 18.5 per cent of graduates earn less than half of the country's median income of $37,002–the highest

proportion of any OECD country, and a phenomenon experts struggle to explain.....
"*Data from the federal Department of Finance show that while fields such as business, engineering and mathematics have returned 12 per cent to 17 per cent a year on education's rising up-front costs, rates for disciplines in the humanities and social sciences could be as low as four per cent to six per cent.*"[13]

And the situation could worsen, as McMaster University economics professor Arthur Sweetman told the *Globe & Mail* reporter:
"*....average returns will go down 'ever so slightly,' as large cohorts graduate into a soft job market.... 'It's clear that there are many people who go to post secondary–10 or 20 per cent–that really don't have wonderful labor market outcomes,' Dr. Sweetman said.*"[14]

In Britain, often a harbinger of things to come for Canada, more than a third of recent
graduates are employed in low-skilled jobs. Reported the Manchester *Guardian*:
"*In the final quarter of 2011, 35.9 per cent of those who had graduated from university in the previous six years were employed in lower-skilled occupations, the Office for National Statistics (ONS) said. This compares with 26.7 per cent, or just over one in four, in 2001.*
"*In the same period, the number of recent graduates in the jobs market has grown by 438,000 to around 1.5 million in 2011.*
"*Jobs categorized as low-skilled by the ONS include hotel porters, waiters and bar staff, and retail assistants.*"[15]

So, yes, university education can provide an advantage in the labor market, but it isn't guaranteed. And to tell students it's worth becoming indentured for most of their adult lives with crippling debt, because they'll make a "million dollars," is, to put it bluntly, a con job.

Graham Cox, of the Canadian Federation of Students, brings the controversy down to earth: "People who graduate do not have a guarantee of an income of the high end. What they have a guarantee of is being part of the average earners in society."

Insh'Allah.

Still another, likely unfruitful, route towards easing the debt disaster is that of piecemeal solutions, tinkering here and there with the system in hopes of temporarily quieting its most vocal critics, but retaining its underlying philosophy. This is the approach taken by various granting schemes, usually involving very modest grants, aimed at a narrow segment of students from low-income families. It's also the approach taken more recently by such schemes as Ontario's tuition rebate plan, mentioned earlier.

Targeting a limited number of grants to the lowest income section of society fails to solve the overall problem, which typically hits the middle class hardest. As Mackenzie noted:

"A strategy of raising tuition and targeting assistance to the lowest-income families will move the financial obstacles to participation in post secondary well into the middle of the income distribution..... Less than 15 per cent of first-year students in Ontario would receive any grant assistance under this structure.

"The Ontario and Canada Access Grants combined will cover only about five per cent of total first-year tuition. The grants fall far short of the true cost of attending university for

low-income students and totally neglect students whose families are in the middle."[16]

Of course, Mackenzie was writing in 2005, and there have been various grant ideas proposed or passed, in various provinces, since then. But the general situation remains consistent. Most grant schemes fail to cover more than a fraction of costs, and often ignore middle-income families. And too often, given the nature of politics and political spin machines, even the tuition relief schemes that do target larger sections of the population, including the beleaguered middle class, are often of the "right hand giveth while the left hand taketh away" variety. Recently, for example, Ontario unveiled a new $420 million tuition rebate plan, trumpeted as benefitting some 300,000 post secondary students. At the same time that it announced this rebate, with fanfare, it quietly moved to offset it by "the elimination of three existing student aid programs:

"1) Ontario Trust for Student Support–a $25 million fund that matches donated institutional scholarships and bursaries;

"2) Textbook and Technology Grant–a $39 million program which provides $150 each year in assistance to all Ontario Student Assistance Plan (OSAP) recipients;

"3) Queen Elizabeth II Aiming for the Top Scholarship–a $35 million scholarship program with 15,000 recipients.

"In addition to Phasing out the three existing student aid programs, another $100 million is expected to be recovered by the government by providing fewer provincial grants and loans."[17]

As if these clawbacks weren't enough, the province also announced it was slashing funding for research projects at universities and hospitals by $66 million. According to reports, the "government withdrew the research funding to free up money for other programs."[18]

Another form of piecemeal solution, offered by critics of the North American student loan system such as U.S. author Alan Collinge, is to ease the burden of student loan debtors by restoring the consumer protections taken away from them by legislators.[19] This would include bankruptcy protections removed in both the U.S. and Canada, as well as statutes of limitations and limits on collection agency powers. Certainly, restoring such protections would make things less harsh for debtors, in the same way that easing parole rules, or improving the diet in prison cafeterias, would make life easier for convicts.

But it would not solve the fundamental problem, namely: that **debt has become an automatic sentence, very much like a prison sentence, for those seeking an education.**

Four sources

So, if the above are false paths, what models could lead to a better way of handling the financing of higher education in Canada?

At least four practical sources of inspiration include:

1) Our own history and traditions;
2) The example of other democratic, developed countries;
3) A proposal by Canada's university teachers, as represented by the Canadian Association of University Teachers (CAUT), which is largely supported by the Canadian Federation of Students (CFS);
4) The post secondary education policy of the country's Official Opposition, the New Democratic Party, including a private member's bill submitted by the NDP

critic for post-secondary education, Rathika Sitsabaiesan.

Since the mid-19th century, when pioneer educators like Ontario's Edgerton Ryerson, Quebec's Jean-Baptiste Meilleur and B.C.'s John Jessup were developing their proposals for public education, free schooling has been considered a basic feature of North American society. Only its duration and religious affiliations, if any, have changed.

At first, when farming was the main occupation and land the chief source of family security, a grounding in the three-Rs seemed sufficient. Later, as manufacturing and the capitalist economy developed, education came to be seen as the basis for prosperity, rather than land. And eventually schooling was made compulsory, first to age 16 and then in some provinces to age 18. A high school diploma came to be seen as the key to employment, and secondary schools featured both academic and vocational, or "shop" courses. The sort of workforce needed to guarantee a healthy economy required secondary school and, whether denominational or secular, education was government supported.

By now regarded as a basic right, it was seen as needed to assure the continuance of those very Canadian values: Peace, Order and Good Government.

There is really nothing new in seeing things this way. What is new is that society, technology and the economies of the world have moved on from simpler times, and today the twin roles of high school shop and academic courses have been taken over by the community college curriculum and, on the academic side, university. As noted earlier in this book, post-secondary education has become the new requirement, for close to three quarters of the jobs available in this country.

To see it also as a right, and wish to assure its availability to any qualified student, regardless of his or her financial status, doesn't require a great leap of imagination, at least in principle. For that matter, as Chapter Six showed, up until the Mulroney years, post secondary schooling was heavily subsidized by government, and what little tuition fees it demanded were within the financial reach of ordinary Canadians. Only in recent decades has it taken on the character of a privilege, to be bestowed only upon the wealthy, or those willing to indenture themselves for a good part of their adult lives.

The idea of offering free, publicly-supported post-secondary education ought to come naturally to Canadians.

As it does, in fact, to the citizens of many other developed countries--such as France, Finland, Norway, Sweden and Denmark--and to those of several Latin American nations, Brazil, and the island of Cuba included.

The French constitution itself declares that it is the duty of the state "to provide free, compulsory, secular education at all levels." As a recent government publication explains:

"The French school system was founded on general principles that were inspired by the 1789 revolution, built on and perfected by a set of legislative texts from the 19th century to the present day.

"State schools and private schools that have a contract with the state coexist within the state system. In exchange for signing a public contract, private schools benefit from state support but are subject to regulation and must respect the national curriculum..... The French school system has been based on the principle of secularism since the end of the 19th century. State schooling has been secular since the Jules Ferry Education Act of 28 March 1882.... The principle of religious freedom led to the introduction of one day off every week to allow for religious teaching outside school."[20]

This author can testify personally to the quality of university education in France, having been a student there himself during part of his own undergraduate years, in the 1960s. Despite being a foreign student, I was able to study tuition-free and ended up spending an entire year there, room and board at a Jesuit-owned hostel included, for a grand total of $1,000. It was one of the best years of my life, and left me with a lasting affinity for French literature, as well as (it goes almost without saying) French cooking.

It left me with no debt, other than one of sincere gratitude.

The Canadian province of Quebec, which too many English Canadians still seem to see as a foreign country, has traditionally followed the French example. Starting with the Parti Quebecois, which in its early days had a genuinely social-democratic orientation, a succession of Quebec governments have acted as if higher education ought to be a right, accessible to all. The province's publicly-funded CEGEP system (for College d'enseignement general et professionnel)—roughly equivalent to community college--is effectively tuition-free, while average university tuition in la belle province is the lowest in Canada.

That is, until recently, when the Liberal government of Jean Charest, adopting the austerity mantra of the far right, imposed a sharp rise in tuition rates, and provoked a massive student backlash. Led by the militant group CLASSE (Coalition Large de l'Association pour une Solidarite Styndicale Etudiante) young Quebeckers took to the streets in what became one of the largest and longest-running political protests in Canadian history.

The English media, especially the conservative business press, portrayed the protesters as spoiled brats, complaining over tuition fees which, even with the Charest hikes, were still among the lowest in the country. What the right wing punditry failed to comprehend was that such finger wagging was, in effect, like ridiculing a mugging victim who lost only $20 to bandits, by pointing out how much more money other holdup victims have lost. The real question was, why weren't the other mugging victims—students in the other provinces—also out in the streets?

Like France, the Scandinavian countries also share a profoundly democratic approach to education, as they do, in fact, to many things in life. In Sweden, for example, students are not only encouraged to participate in activities like student government, but also to help plan and develop their own course of studies. In consultation with teachers, they choose what books to read and how to balance practice with theory in a given subject area. Tuition is free at all levels, including university, although there are a handful of boarding schools, or "private schools," funded by privately paid tuition.

In Norway and Denmark, public education is also tuition-free, including university education. And Denmark takes this a step further, covering students' living expenses while enrolled, via a monthly stipend. All Danish students who are Danish citizens are given *Statens Uddannelsesstotte* (state support) of 2,728 Danish kroners per month, if living with their parents, and 5,486 kroners if living away from family.[21] Danes can supplement the monthly stipend with low-interest government loans of up to 2,807 kroners.

The thinking behind this generous program was explained by a spokes person for the Danish ministry of education:

"The initial reason is to ensure equal access to education for all students, in spite of parental income," said Charlotte Rohlin, adding with refreshing clarity that the real "starting point is political values. We have free education because that is what the politicians want, and they want it because the population wants it."[22]

Any doubts about what the population wants were dispelled during the brief, recent tenure in power of the country's right wing party. "At the end of the late centre-right government's run, there was a large debate about the possibility of introducing tuition at Danish universities," said Rohlin. "The [then] Opposition accused the government of intending to introduce tuition, and demanded that it not happen. The result was that all parties [came out] against introducing tuition." And the right-tending party fell from power not long afterward.

On a purely kroners-and-pence basis, she added that numerous studies had also "looked into both returns [for investment in education] on a private and at a public level. The studies show that there are positive returns to public investment in tertiary education when they take into account .... that well educated people have a higher likelihood of being employed, tend to earn more [and thus pay higher taxes], are less frequently ill [requiring less public expenditure for health care], etc."

Indeed, the OECD has looked at the question of public returns in depth, via a survey of all 31 of its member countries (Canada being one), and published the results in the report mentioned earlier. According to the report:

"The net public return is almost three times the cost of investing in tertiary education, which means there is a strong incentive for governments to expand higher education. As with returns to individuals, the benefits to the public purse are higher when people complete tertiary rather than upper secondary education.

"The economic benefits of education flow not just to individuals but also to governments through additional tax receipts when people enter the labor market....

"For the public sector, the costs of education include direct expenditures on education (such as paying teachers' salaries), public-private transfers, and lost tax revenues on students' forgone earnings [if they don't work while studying]. The benefits include increased revenue from income taxes and social insurance payments on higher wages as well as a lower need for social transfers. But in practice, rising levels of education give rise to a much wider–and more complex–set of fiscal effects on the benefit side. For instance, better educated individuals generally have better health, which lowers public expenditure on provision of health care. Also, their earnings premium means they spend more on goods and services, which has wider economic benefits."[23]

It doesn't take a rocket scientist to understand the logic. It's the same logic that makes it obvious that a flatlining economy, in need of the kind of stimulus that only increased consumer spending can offer, won't get that stimulus if an entire generation of consumers are so debt-ridden after finishing school that they can't buy cars, or houses, or start families as their parents generation did in a less education-hostile, bank-and-bill-collector-friendly, society.

Walter Reuther, co-founder of the United Auto Workers union (parent of the Canadian Auto Workers Union), was once in a bargaining session with representatives of the Big Three U.S. automakers, who were in the process of automating several key manufacturing plants. After listening to several presentations on the savings automation would bring, he tapped a pencil on the table, and reminded the bargainers of a very basic reality: "Robots don't buy cars."

Nor do people whose outstanding debts are already expressed in five or six figures.

Teachers and students
When it comes to university education, it's difficult to imagine anyone more familiar with the subject than university teachers and students. The campus is their everyday reality, which is one reason why it might be worth considering what they have to say.

The Canadian Association of University Teachers (CAUT) has for years been advocating for change in the post-secondary system, not only in how it is financed, but also how it is governed. While respecting the fact that the rules of Confederation make education a provincial responsibility, they also see the weakness of having no national consensus, no consistent, nationwide set of standards, and depending for school funding–even where federal social transfer payments are involved--on the vagaries of the shifting political winds in each individual province. The amount of money in the social transfer may be set in Ottawa, as bloc funding, but how, or even if it is used is currently decided in each provincial legislature.

In an attempt to remedy these difficulties, while respecting Confederation's division of powers, the CAUT has come up with a proposed *Canada Post-Secondary Education Act*. The bill's introduction outlines the problems:

"The future of post-secondary education in Canada is at a crossroads. After years of public funding cuts, the quality and accessibility of universities and colleges is at risk. Skyrocketing tuition fees, fewer faculty, larger classes, fewer course offerings, reduced library holdings, and the commercialization of research are all symptomatic of the continuing and chronic public under-funding of post-secondary education.

"Compounding the lack of adequate public funding are fundamental flaws in federal-provincial fiscal arrangements in support of post-secondary education. The Canada Social Transfer (CST) provides no accountability as to how federal

transfers are allocated by the provinces and in turn has allowed Ottawa to offload its responsibilities in the area. These flaws in the design of the CST have allowed the two levels of government to bicker over funding arrangements and jurisdiction, while support for universities and colleges has fallen through the cracks.

"Given these problems, CAUT believes there is an urgent need to reconsider not just the level of funding, but also the mechanism and rules by which the federal government provides support for colleges and universities."[24]

The proposed Act would contain:

"1) A declaration that the legislation does not alter or encroach upon the provinces' jurisdiction over post-secondary education;

"2) A statement of the financial responsibility of Parliament for the support of post-secondary education and the establishment of a stable funding arrangement."[25]

The Act's key elements would include:

"a) the repeal of the CST and the establishment of a National Post-Secondary Education Fund to provide stable federal cash funding.... The cash value of the Post-Secondary Education Fund would initially be set at 0.3 per cent of GDP (roughly doubling current spending) and would rise to 0.5 per cent (about the same level it was in the late 1970s and early 1980s) within two years, where it would remain. To ensure regional equality, cash transfers to the provinces will be allocated on a per capita basis and equalized according to provincial GDP per capita.

"b) The establishment of national principles setting standards for the provision of post-secondary education.... on the following basis:
"* public administration–a post-secondary education system that is provided on a public and not-for-profit basis;
"* accessibility–post-secondary education should be open to all qualified persons on uniform terms and conditions;
"* collegial governance–post-secondary education institutions should be governed in a collegial manner which includes meaningful and effective representation from faculty and students;
"* comprehensiveness–a post-secondary education system that provides faculty and students with a full range of academic programs;
"* academic freedom–assure protection of the principle of free and independent academic inquiry and the academic and intellectual autonomy of post-secondary institutions.
"c) The creation of an arm's length advisory council on post-secondary education. The council would include broad representation from both levels of government and the academic community. The council would advise the Minister of Human Resources and Development and present yearly reports to Parliament."[26]

Finally, in recognition of the unique "Quebec-Canada relationship," the proposed Act would include "special arrangements with Quebec which may not be open to other provinces."[27]

Obviously, the CAUT proposal is only that–a proposal–and actual passage of such an act would require extensive political negotiation. For example, when the proposed act mentions "stable federal funding," it leaves open several questions that might be asked about the "how much." Its percent-of-GDP formula for a National Post-Secondary Education Fund might look paltry to those who would like to see all post-secondary education become tuition-free, while it might look over-generous to others. The question of how much the provinces ought to contribute to the overall post-secondary financial base is also left open.

But it is at least a starting point, and both the Canadian Federation of Students and the New Democratic Party would like to see the bargaining begin.

"We're the only industrialized country that doesn't have an act at the federal level around post-secondary education," says CFS National Researcher Graham Cox. "We've endorsed the CAUT proposal and are calling for the federal government to implement it."

"It comes back to the British North America Act and its division of powers, where education was written into the provincial column," says CFS National Chairman David Molenhuis. "Health care was also written into the provincial side, but we still managed to come up with a decent public health care system, with federal regulation and provincial administration. So the precedent exists. We need an educational equivalent of the Canada Health Act."

The New Democratic Party, now Canada's official federal Opposition, supports such a move. In fact, Rathika Sitsabaiesan, MP for Scarborough-Rouge River and the NDP's post-secondary education critic, submitted a private member's bill in June 2011, Bill C-265.[28] Similar in many respects to the CAUT's proposed Canada Post-Secondary Education Act, it would replace the current Canada Social Transfer (CST) bloc payment, and set federal funding for colleges and universities apart from funding for other social services.

Like the CAUT's proposed act, it would create a standing committee for administration of the act, and require an annual report to Parliament. It would also create a set of national standards, binding on all provinces, regarding academic freedom, student-to-faculty ratios, accreditation, and equality of student access to higher education. And, like the CAUT proposal, it would leave open to negotiation any special requirements for the province of Quebec.

How much the federal payments might total, in dollar terms, and whether they would be sufficient, with provincial contributions, to provide a tuition-free system like those of Western Europe, is left open in both model acts.

In politics, one must sometimes move forward in small increments.

The basic question

Can we afford to create a system of tuition-free post-secondary education in Canada? This is the basic question posed, however disingenuously, by austerity advocates.

To which a fair reply might be, can we afford not to?

Can we afford to continue financially hobbling graduates from our community colleges and universities–except those from very rich families–to the point where the only contribution they can make to the economy is to continue paying the interest on student loans many can never hope to discharge, or to sacrifice a decade or more of their working lives to pay off the principal? Should all other economic activity in Canada grind slowly to a halt, while future generations focus solely on enriching banks, or getting the Canada Revenue Agency off their backs?

Robots don't buy cars.

DEBT SENTENCE

Our neighbors to the south have gotten many things wrong in recent years, and their economy and politics are in deep disarray. If anything, their system of educational finance is worse than ours: American student loan debt–now at $946 billion--recently surpassed total consumer credit card debt. But a refreshing suggestion came recently from the border state of Michigan, where Democratic members of the State Senate proposed a plan to provide free tuition for Michigan post-secondary students. According to news reports:

"Hoping to refocus priorities in 2012, the state's Senate Democrats have released a new plan that puts Michigan students ahead of wealthy corporations.

"Under the Michigan 2020 Plan, Michigan's high school graduates will be eligible for free tuition at one of Michigan's community colleges or universities, where the median tuition level is currently around $9,575 per year. The program will be funded entirely by eliminating $3.5 billion in tax credits and loopholes [for corporations] and putting that money towards students.

"'Study after study has emphasized the importance of a highly educated workforce in the economic vitality of any state in the 21st century,' said Senate Democratic leader Gretchen Whitmer, D-East Lansing.

"Michigan currently pays out roughly $34 billion in tax credits. Under the Michigan 2020 Plan recently unveiled, $3.5 billion in tax credits and loopholes would be eliminated. Democrats put the tuition proposal's cost at $1.8 billion.

"Under the plan, graduates who spent their entire K-12 years in Michigan schools would be eligible for the full award, which equates to the median tuition level of all public universities....

"Senate Democrats note that the elimination of $3.5 billion in tax loopholes is only a 10 per cent reduction in the tax

credits the state already doles out. In fact, the program costs almost exactly as much as the $1.7 billion tax cut [Michigan Governor] Snyder implemented for corporations.

"The plan should appeal to Republicans as 'it can be done without raising taxes one cent,' said Whitmer. 'It's not about whether Michigan can afford to do this. It's whether we can afford not to.'"[29]

Took the words right out of my mouth........

If tiny Denmark can manage to assure its children a debt-free education, because "the population wants it," we certainly can. We owe it to our kids.

And what of those who are already enmeshed in the student loan trap? A new national policy that provides free tuition, and national standards for education, won't free them from present indenture, or repair the damage done to thousands of lives and careers across the nation. Nor will it–until the first crop of liberated students graduates and takes its place in society–do anything to stimulate an economy that needs to get off life support now.

CanadaStudentDebt website founder Mark O'Meara responds to that question. After watching the tortured workings of our current system for many years, and having been its one-time victim, he makes no bones about it:

"The student loan system is so badly broken, that all previous loans should be forgiven and erased from credit bureau reporting and the government should issue an apology to those harmed by the incompetence of the National Student Loans Service Centre, the banks and the collection agencies that abused borrowers. The forgiveness of loans would be a great boost to the economy, as it would allow our younger generation to put money towards housing, saving for retirement, or other purchases that would bring abundance to our economy."[30]

After interviewing dozens of students for this book, including many who couldn't be quoted by name or who talked to me off-the-record, as well as witnessing the hardships visited upon my own students in the 10 years I spent in the classroom, I'm tempted to go O'Meara one better, and say there is a case, at least in some instances, for reparations to be paid to those who were damaged by the system. Though different in nature, the example of the sad history of First Nations victims of residential schools provides a partial precedent.

Perhaps the Occupy Movement may consider taking up such a cause.

We would also do well to consider returning our institutions of higher learning to the goals in which they once gloried: the search for truth for its own sake, and the education of our youth for their sakes. Making a buck cannot be the basis for such an endeavor.

A recent essay on this subject is worth quoting:

"The truly educated become conscious. They become self-aware. They do not lie to themselves. They do not pretend fraud is moral or that corporate agreed is good. They do not claim that the demands of the marketplace can morally justify the hunger of children or denial of medical care to the sick. They do not throw six million families from their homes as the cost of doing business.

"Thought is a dialogue with one's inner self. Those who think ask questions, questions those in authority do not want asked. They remember who we are, where we come from and where we should go. They remain eternally skeptical and distrustful of power. And they know that this moral independence is the only protection from the radical evil that results from collective unconsciousness. The capacity to think is the only bulwark against any centralized authority that seeks to impose mindless obedience. There is a huge difference, as

Socrates understood, between teaching people what to think, and teaching them how to think."[31]

1. Bob Rae, "Ontario: a leader in learning," (Toronto: Government of Ontario, February 2005).

2. For example: Alex Usher, "The price of knowledge 2002" and "The price of knowledge 2004," Canadian Millennium Scholarship Foundation.

3. Hugh Mackenzie, Hugh Mackenzie & Associates, "The tuition trap," September 2005, a study commissioned by the Ontario Confederation of University Faculty Associations (OCUFA).

4. Robert Benzie and Tanya Talaga, "Drummond Report: roadmap for a more austere Ontario set for release today," 15 February 2012, The Toronto *Star*, as posted online at http://www.thestar.com/printarticle/1131603

5. James Bradshaw, "Schools and universities should consider user fees and tuition hikes: Drummond," 15 February 2012, *The Globe & Mail*, as posted online at http://www.theglobeandmail.com/news/national/education/universityn...

6. Murray Dobbin, "Why Flaherty loves his $50 billion deficit," 1 June 2009, *The Tyee*, as posted online at http://thetyee.ca/Views/2009/06/01/FedDeficit/print.html

7. Bill Berkowitz, "Class warfare in Canada orchestrated by right-wing Prime Minister Harper," 2 December 2011, *The Buzzflash Blog*, as posted online at http://blog.buzzflash.com/node/13187

8. Ontario Public Service Employees Union (OPSEU), "Drummond Report: how to manufacture a crisis," 17 February 2012, *Diablogue*, as posted online at http://diablogue.org/2012/02/17/drummond-report-how-to-manufacture...

9. OPSEU, *Op. Cit.*

10. Ann Pettifor, "Standard & Poor's is right, 'austerity' has no economic clothes," 6 December 2011, *The Guardian*, as posted online at http://www.guardian.co.uk/commentisfree/2011/dec/06/standard-and-p...

11. Mackenzie, *Op. Cit.*, 17-21.

12. Organization for Economic Coooperation and Development (OECD), "Highlights from Education at a Glance 2010," *OECD Publishing* 2010, 42.

13. James Bradshaw, "Bachelor's degree no guarantee of earnings success," 25 September 2011, The Toronto *Globe & Mail*, as posted online at http://www.theglobeandmail.com/news/national/education/universityn...

14. Bradshaw, *Op. Cit.*

15. Graham Snowdon, "A third of recent graduates in unskilled jobs," 6 March 2012, *The Guardian*, as posted online at http://www.guardian.co.uk/money/2012/mar/06/recent-graduates-emp...

16. Mackenzie, *Op. Cit.*, 4.

17. Krystal Yee, "Check out Ontario's new tuition tax break," 9 January 2012, Moneyville, as posted online at http://www.moneyville.ca/print/1112425

18. Karen Howlett, "Ontario universities, hospitals 'in shock' after $66 million funding cut," 9 January 2012, The *Globe & Mail*, as posted online at http://www.theglobeandmail.com/news/national/education/universityn...

19. Alan Michael Collinge, "Commentary: a plea to add consumer protections to student Loans," 11 January 2010, The New York *Times*, as posted online at http://thechoice.blogs.nytimes.com/2010/01/11/bankruptcy/?pagemode...

20. Republique Francaise, ministere de l'education nationale, "School Education in France 2010," Paris, 2010, 4.

21. *Wikipedia, the free encyclopedia*, "Education in Denmark," 2, as posted online 2 March 2012, at http://en.wikipedia.org/wiki/Education_in_Denmark

22. Charlotte Rohlin Blastrup, Chefkonsulent, Kontoret for Statens Uddannelsesstotte, Ministeriet for Forskning, Innovation og Videregaende Uddannelser, Denmark, personal communication, 5 January 2012.

23. OECD, *Op. Cit.*, 44.

24. Canadian Association of University Teachers (CAUT),

"Canada Post-Secondary Education Act," Ottawa, 2007, Introduction, i.

25. Act, *Op. Cit.*, ii.

26. *Op. Cit.*, ii-iii.

27. *Loc. Cit.*

28. Rathika Sitsabaiesan, House of Commons of Canada, Bill C-265, 23 June 2011, available at the Parliament of Canada website, http://www.parl.gc.ca

29. Tonya Somanader, "Michigan Democrats unveil plan to finance free college tuition by eliminating corporate tax credits," 17 January 2012, *Truthout*, as posted online at http:www.truth-out.org/print/11622

30. Mark O'Meara, "Policy of this site," *CanadaStudentDebt.ca*, as posted online at http://www.canadastudentdebt.ca/sitepolicy.asp

31. Chris Hedges, "Why the United States is destroying its education system," 11 April 2011, *Truthout*, as posted online at http://truthout.org/print/905

Chapter Nine: Sources, Tools, Allies

"I am armed, and well prepared."

--Shakespeare, *The Merchant of Venice*

An old dictum has it that before you can defeat an enemy, "you must first know who he is." It's a good idea also to know who your friends are.

The student loan system, as it functions today, seems a friend to few. Whatever its purpose may have been in the past, to thousands of Canadians it now looks mostly like an engine of entrapment and indenture. Students should regard it as their last resort, not the first. And if they find they must make use of it, that there is no other way to fund their education, they should know what they are facing.

The obvious relief of one contributor to the CanadaStudentDebt.ca website, upon finally getting the student loan monkey off his back, should stand as a warning:

"This might be my final post on this website. As of a few weeks ago I finally paid off my student loans in full. My final confirmation of payment in full arrived in the mail about a week and a half ago.

"The freedom feels great!

"Never again will I walk into a [Bank R] branch to make a student loan payment.

"Never again will I take out another student loan.

"My wife and I have been preparing our children for post-secondary education. As long as they live under our roof, they

are required to give 50 per cent of their employment income to us, which we put away in a special account for their education. We will do as much as we can to ensure that they will not need to take out a student loan as they pursue an education.

"I will always warn parents whose children want to take out student loans that the banks are NOT their friend when it comes to education funding: they are interested in making money.

"Hang in there......."

Following is a list of information sources, some general, some historical and some practical, other than those provided by the people who currently control the system.

Historical background
John Henry Newman. *The Idea of a University.* Notre Dame, Indiana: University of Notre Dame Press, 2009.

A classic exposition of the goals and purposes of higher education, this book, based on a series of lectures in Dublin in 1852, has inspired both secular and religious theorists. It stands in direct opposition to the philosophy that education is no more than a profit-making business geared towards training people to get jobs.

Ross Finnie and Saul Schwartz. *Student loans in Canada: past, present and future*, Toronto: C.D. Howe Institute, 1996.

Though dated, this book gives an excellent summary of the evolution of Canada's system of financing post-secondary education up to the late 1990s, including valuable statistics, tables, charts and political background. Essential for the long view.

Alan Michael Collinge. *The Student loan scam: the most oppressive debt in U.S. history–and how we can fight back.* Boston: Beacon Press, 2009.
Though focused on the U.S. system, much of Collinge's information applies equally well to Canada. Notable for its political insight and inside views of the loans and collections industry.

James D. Scurlock. *Maxed Out: hard times, easy credit, and the era of predatory lenders.* New York: Scribner, 2007.
A good, old-fashioned journalistic expose of the consumer loan industry in the U.S., with special attention to the outrageous and the predatory. A best-seller in the U.S., the book was later made into a film documentary of the same title. A wonderful illustration of the saying *caveat emptor:* let the buyer beware.

Canadian Federation of Students. *Money Does Matter: an alternative for accessible, high quality post-secondary education.* Ottawa: Canadian Federation of Students, October 2007.
A well-researched, bilingual overview of the current system of student financing, from the viewpoint of the 700,000-member Canadian Federation of Students. The CFS is an independent organization, not affiliated with any parent body or political party, which functions much as a labor union for students.

Canadian Federation of Students. *Public Education for the Public Good: a national vision for Canada's post-secondary education system.* Ottawa: Canadian Federation of Students, 2011.

A bilingual outline, with charts and statistics, of the CFS vision for a legislative and financial framework for higher education.

Organization for Economic Cooperation and Development (OECD). *Highlights from Education at a Glance 2010.* Paris: OECD Publishing, 2010.
An in-depth description of all aspects of education, including how it is financed, in the 31 OECD member nations, including Canada. Chock full of graphs, tables and reliable statistics.

Reports, papers and shorter publications
Canadian Association of University Teachers (CAUT). *CAUT Almanac of Post-Secondary Education in Canada, 2011-2012.* Ottawa: Canadian Association of University Teachers, 2012.
A meticulously detailed description of Canada's system of higher education, including colleges, universities and libraries, replete with charts and statistics, nationally and by province.
Published annually.

National Graduate Caucus. *Public Risk, Private Gain: an introduction to the commercialization of university research.* Ottawa: Canadian Federation of Students (CFS), 2009.
A well-researched discussion of the pitfalls of conducting university research as a purely profit-making business.

Mark O'Meara. *Canada student loans: the need for change.* Vancouver: CanadaStudentDebt.ca, 1 November 2007.
A thoughtful, well-founded overview of what's wrong with our current student loan system, as seen by the moderator of

Canada's preeminent national website devoted to student loan issues. O'Meara is a keen observer, and at the time of writing was far ahead of most other student loan critics. His thinking has evolved since publication of this paper, and is now, once again, ahead of most (see below for website information).

Hugh Mackenzie. *The Tuition Trap.* Toronto: Hugh Mackenzie & Associates, September 2005.

A well-researched study, commissioned by the Ontario Confederation of University Faculty Associations (OCUFA), of the effects of rising tuition fees on university and college accessibility.

Pamela Burdman. *The student debt dilemma: debt aversion as a barrier to college access.* Berkeley, Calif.: Center for Studies in Higher Education, University of California at Berkeley, October 2005.

A landmark study, which showed, among other things, that for every $1,000 rise in university tuition, there is a corresponding 10 per cent drop in participation by students from low-income families.

Office of the Chief Actuary, Superintendent of Financial Institutions Canada, *Actuarial Report of the Canada Student Loans Program, as at 31 July 2009.* Ottawa: Office of the Chief Actuary, 2009.

A bilingual compendium of statistics, published annually, of the activities of the Canada Student Loans Program.

Department of Justice Canada. *Canada Student Loans Act/Regulations (R.S., 1985, c. S-23).* Ottawa: Department of

Justice Canada, 2011. As posted online at http://laws.justice.gc.ca/en/S-23/
The law governing the Canadian Student Loans Program.

Department of Justice Canada. Bankruptcy and Insolvency Act (Chapter B-3). Ottawa: Department of Justice Canada, 14 December 2010. As posted online at http://laws-lois.justice.gc.ca
The law regarding student loan bankruptcy.

Websites/Internet groups
CanadaStudentDebt.ca
Canada's premier website devoted to discussion and resolution by borrowers of student loan difficulties. Moderated by Mark O'Meara. There is a real spirit of mutual support and community on this gem of a site, which has been operating for more than a decade.

Organizations
Canadian Federation of Students
338 Somerset St. W.
Ottawa, Ontario
K2P 0J9
tel. (613) 232-7394
fax. (613) 232-0276
e-mail: info@cfs-fcee.ca
web: www.cfs-fcee.ca

The largest independent body uniting post-secondary students from across Canada, with member locals on most campuses. Militant and progressive, it has its own research staff and publications division, and advocates for fairness and accessibility to higher education for all Canadians. Its current membership is approximately 700,000.

Legal advice
Student borrowers experiencing difficulty with student loan debt and looking for legal advice should contact their campus CFS affiliate group, which may know of local lawyers who work with students, or contact the various provincial Law Societies, such as the Law Society of Upper Canada or the Law Society of British Columbia, most of which operate lawyer referral services.

For a nominal fee, such referral services will provide names of lawyers specializing in such areas as bankruptcy, consumer protection and the like, who may offer an initial half-hour consultation.

Those for whom legal fees are a serious financial barrier should contact Legal Aid offices in their areas or on campus. Some law faculties make legal aid available to students in difficulty.

Debt Counselors
Another source of help for student borrowers who encounter difficulties is the debt counseling business. These agencies specialize in helping borrowers to consolidate and manage loan debts, and aid them in navigating the loans bureaucracy. Some of these agencies are very good, and do help. Others see borrowers as targets, to be milked for their money. All are in business and must make a profit to survive.

Borrowers should look for agencies that focus specifically on student loans, rather than general or credit card debt. As to which are good and which not, it's a matter of one's personal judgment. The old adage holds: *caveat emptor*, let the buyer beware.